HORSE IDENTIFIER

HORSE IDENTIFIER

Sterling Publishing Co., Inc.

A QED BOOK

Published in 1980 by Sterling Publishing Co., Inc.
Two Park Avenue, New York, N.Y. 10016

Original edition published in Great Britain under
the title
Horse by Horse

ISBN 0 8069 3742 4
Library of Congress Catalog Card Number
80-50439

Printed in Hong Kong by Leefung Asco Ltd.

This book is based on some of the material
from The Complete Book of the Horse. It was
designed and produced by QED Publishing
Limited, 32 Kingly Court, London W1
Editorial Director Jeremy Harwood
Art Director Alastair Campbell
Production Director Edward Kinsey
Art Editor David Mallott
Art and editorial co-ordination Heather Jackson
Illustrators Kai Choi, Harry Clow,
Christopher Forsey, Tony Graham, Rory
Kee, Elaine Keenan, Edwina Keene, Abdul
Aziz Khan, Kathleen McDougall, Martin
Woodford, Kathy Wyatt, David Staples,
Jim Marks.
Technical Consultants
Pamela MacGregor-Morris, Jane Kidd.

Contents

Introduction

Throughout history, the horse has been one of the closest animals to man; today, with the great interest in horses shown by people of all ages, the bond is becoming ever closer.

The structure of the book

This book is designed to answer some of the basic questions such people ask about the horse: where did it originate and how did it evolve into the animal we know today? How is it physically made? What are the characteristics of the many breeds of horse in the world and how do they differ in character as well as appearance? The chapter on Evolution takes the story of the horse from the emergence of the so-called 'dawn horse' over 55 million years of geological time until the evolution of *Equus*. The Points of the Horse chapter examines the animal's physical make-up, while the section on the Breeds of the World covers the horses concerned according to geographic area and then proceeds to detailed examination of individual breeds through illustration and extensive captions. For ease of reference, the bulk of this section is in alphabetical order.

A good horse

What makes a good horse is a question debated by riders all over the world and it is one to which there is no single answer. There is no doubt, however, that correct breeding is one of the most important

factors. This is a complex business a should never be undertaken lightly; the very top of the scale, breeding is multi-million dollar and pound indust while, even at the domestic level, it c still be an extremely expensi undertaking. Firstly, it is vital that be parents are of as sound a stock possible, though, in some cases, 1 virtues of a stallion can be used to corre some of the faults of the mare.

The stages of pregnancy

Having decided to breed, the next ster to choose a suitable stud. Mares co into season at regular intervals betwe eighteen and twenty-one days; it is at tl time that they can be 'serve (inseminated) by a stallion. After this h taken place, most studs keep the mare 1 about six weeks to ensure as far possible that the animal concerned h 'held' to the service. This is check again through veterinary examination blood and urine samples at a later dat Before the mare is even accepted by t stud, a veterinary certificate is usua required, guaranteeing that the animal free from disease and infection.

Mating itself takes only a couple minutes, but the preparations can last 1 much longer. At many studs a lowe grade stallion called a 'teaser' is kept try mares in order to establish wheth they are ready for service. During t actual process itself, both mare a stallion are kept firmly under control l stud grooms. To aid in this, both a bridled throughout.

Pregnancy lasts for approximate eleven months. During this time, tl mare needs little extra care, apart fron slightly richer diet. Provided that she ot over-exerted, she can be safely ridden to an advanced stage of pregnancy — to a maximum of seven months as exercise is good for all pregnant animals.

Ponies are often thought to foal best in the field, as they do in the wild; the more well-bred the breed, however, the more attention that will be necessary. Again, the best thing to do is to book the mare into a stud well in advance of the expected birth date. There, she will receive expert care and constant supervision — many of the best studs, for instance, now have closed-circuit television to help in this task.

Birth and after

The first signs of labour are when the mare begins to pace around restlessly, swishing her tail and glancing at her sides. Wax forms on the udder and drops of the teats. As the labour pains intensify, the mare lies down. Birth is imminent when she releases her waters — that is, when the membranes of the sack containing the foal and its protective fluid break.

Delivery itself usually presents few problems, unless the foal is abnormally presented. This can occur if, say, the hind end is presented foremost — what is known as a breech presentation. In most cases, manipulation is the answer and this is why it is always preferable to have an expert on call. Again taking the example of breech presentation, it is essential to make sure that both the hind legs are in the birth passage. This must be done quickly, as otherwise the umbilical cord supplying air to the foal can become trapped. If this happens, the foal will drown in the fluid contained in the protective membrane.

When birth has been completed, the mare recovers swiftly in almost all cases. So, too, does the foal; after an initial licking by its mother, it will stand and start to suckle from her teats. This first suck is all important, as the milk contains vitamin-rich colostrum, which gives the foal natural imunity against several juvenile diseases. It also stimulates the bowels into action.

Provided no problems have arisen, mare and foal can both be turned out for exercise a day after the birth. A couple of days after that, the first steps in the foal's training can begin, when a small head collar, known as a slip, is put on the animal. This enables the owner to accustom the foal to being led and handled — the latter is essential if, say, injections are necessary. Slowly, too, it can be given solid food

Life progresses in a regular routine until the foal is ready to be weaned. The best way to do this is to separate it from its mother and keep it in a loose box for two weeks. Solid food should by now be readily accepted; milk pellets can be added if the animal appears to be loosing condition. After this, the foal has to get used to a new routine of field by day and loose box by night. It helps if a companion can be provided as a substitute for the mother — another foal is best — but it is also important to keep the two animals separate at feeding times.

This pattern of life continues for a year or so — the time spent outdoors increasing as the foal gets tougher — until the time comes for it to be broken. The only additional precaution necessary is a regular check on the feet in case of disease.

The Evolution of the Horse

The horse as we know it today is the product of a long evolutionary chain stretching back for literally thousands of years. Before the end of the Ice Age, some 12,000 to 15,000 years ago, the ancestors of present-day *Equus Caballos* roamed the world's grassy plains. These, in turn, emerged as a result of a process spanning some 55 million years of geological time.

The 'dawn horse'

The first of these ancestors was *Eohippus* or *Hyracotherium* (the latter is the accepted scientific name), which flourished from some 55 to 38 million years ago and is considered the first distinct horse. This breed was small in stature — about the size of a fox terrier — but was a notable advance over its own *condylarth* ancestors. The chief difference was the number of digits in each foot — *Hyracotherium* had four on the fore feet and three on the hind, as opposed to the five of the *condylarths*. Its legs were also longer, while the animal's teeth, jaws and skull were deeper and longer than those of its predecessors, making it more suited to grazing. Longer limbs, for their part, meant that *Hyracotherium's* pace was increased, an especially important factor in its battle for survival against its various predator enemies. In addition, recent research has shown that the brain of *Hyracotherium* and other early horses were progressive in their evolution, when compared with other primitive mammals, such as their *condylarth* relatives.

Hyracotherium was also geographical widespread; traces of it have been found both the New and the Old Worlds.

From four toes to three

About 38 million years ago, the first three toed horses emerged, developing from on strain of *Hyracotherium* as the others di out. There were two groups of these - primitive browsers, feeding on lea vegetation, and advanced grazers, feedir on grass. The browsers emerged first - they became extinct about 11 million yea ago — to be followed later by the grazers.

Both groups were bigger than *Hyr*

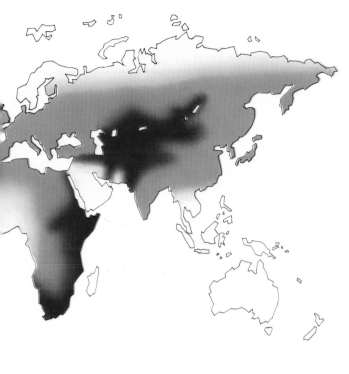

How Equus was distributed during the Pleistocene Epoch and where it is found in the wild today. Equus originated some 3-4 million years ago and spread from its North American homeland to many parts of the world. At the end of the last Ice Age, however, many varieties became extinct, possibly because of climatic change. The distribution of wild Equus today is relatively limited.

therium; both had longer legs; and both d even more effective means of eating. ke *Hyracotherium,* too, they spread dely, starting in North America to reach e Old World some 20 million years ago. t, it was the development of the grazers an independent entity that made this riod an especially important one in horse story, for the change represented an portant diversification of feeding habits the evolutionary process. Specialized azing meant that teeth, skull and jaws d to adapt to cope with the increased ar and tear of chewing abrasive grasses; cordingly all of them became deeper as

time went by.

The main home of these grazers was in North America, though one group — the *Hipparions* — successfully migrated from the New World to the Old some 10 to 11 million years ago. It was on the grassy plains of North America, too, that the first one-toes horses emerged around 15 million years ago.

The emergence of Equus
The first one-toed horses were grazers, like their three-toed ancestors, though they apparently emerged from only one type in North America. This transition from three

9

toes to one was a natural evolutionary consequence, as the size of the side digits gradually became smaller until only the central one played any part in running. On the whole, these horses were bigger bodied than their predecessors, while their molars, skull and jaws were also enlarged.

Most of these one-toed horses were located in Central and North America and it was in the American north that the first representatives of *Equus* developed. These were descended from the one-toed *Dinohippus* and emerged between three and four million years ago. They spread quickly, becoming the most geographically diverse of of all ancestral horses; North, Central and South America, Asia, Europe and Africa all had their colonies. They also consisted of many different species, though, in common with many other large mammals, most of these became extinct by the end of the last Ice Age, about 12,000 to 15,000 years ago.

The reasons for this sudden drastic decline are obscure. Some experts think it was due to the change in climate or the influence of man, while others suggest a combination of these or still more factors. Whatever the cause, the process was severe — particularly in America, the ancestral home of *Equus.* There, horses totally vanished from the scene; they were not to reappear until the Spanish *conquistadores* landed in Mexico in the early 16th century AD.

From the wild to domestication

By the end of this period, *Equus* had reached a recognisably modern form. During this long evolutionary progress, several trends had become apparent — all a direct result of the constant battle for survival in a sometimes hostile environ-ment. On the whole, horses gradua increased in size, though there were tim when some remained the same size or ev grew smaller. Changes in skull and lim also took place, as horses adapted to bet suit themselves for grazing and running

The next major step was the work of external force — that of man. In arou 3000 BC, probably in Asiatic Russia, t horse was first domesticated. The or major area of controversy here is whethe single type of horse was involved whether several types were domest ated at the same time. Some experts belie that two distinct kinds — the now extir tarpan and Przewalski's horse we involved — but others argue that the one related to the other.

In any event, what is certain is that, fro there, the knowledge of domesticati spread rapidly and widely;

The source of knowledge

The evolution of the horse is a fascinati and complex subject that today attra scientists all over the world. The maj source of knowledge is based on the ri fossil deposits of western North America though the first description of *Hydr cotherium* was in fact based on the fin made in the marshes around London 1839. The discovery, made by the Briti paleontologist Sir Richard Owen, d much to inspire the work of successors the field, particularly in the USA.

Chief amongst these scientists was O. Marsh, the Professor of Paleontology Yale University in the Mid-nineteen century. It was Marsh who discover *Eohippus* — the 'dawn horse' — the olde horse in North America. And it was on h work that others built to create much of th knowledge that we possess today.

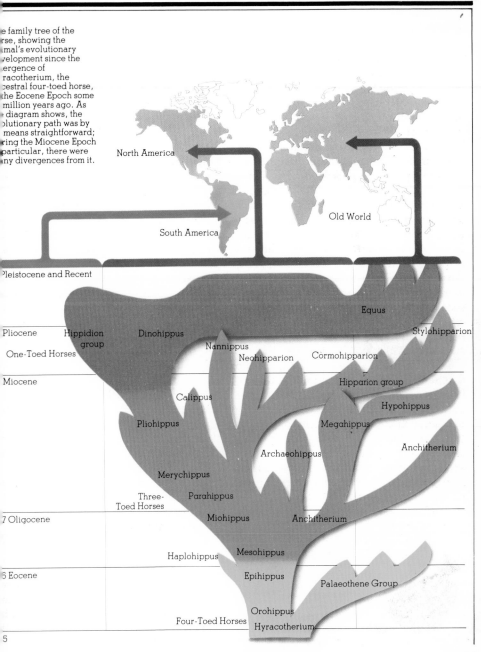

The family tree of the horse, showing the animal's evolutionary development since the emergence of Hyracotherium, the ancestral four-toed horse, in the Eocene Epoch some million years ago. As the diagram shows, the evolutionary path was by no means straightforward; during the Miocene Epoch in particular, there were many divergences from it.

North America

South America

Old World

Pleistocene and Recent

Pliocene

One-Toed Horses

Miocene

Three-Toed Horses

7 Oligocene

6 Eocene

Four-Toed Horses

Equus

Hippidion group

Dinohippus

Nannippus

Neohipparion

Cormohipparion

Stylohipparion

Hipparion group

Calippus

Hypohippus

Pliohippus

Megahippus

Anchitherium

Archaeohippus

Merychippus

Parahippus

Miohippus

Anchitherium

Mesohippus

Haplohippus

Epihippus

Palaeothene Group

Orohippus

Hyracotherium

5

11

The Points of the Horse

Some of the common body colours of the horse. The commonest are bay, chestnut, black and brown, though there are many possible varieties within these broad definitions. Thoroughbreds can be bay/brown, grey and roan, for instance; non-Thoroughbreds can be dun, cream, piebald, odd-coloured, palomino skewbald and so on. In doubtful cases, colouring is officially defined according to that of the points — the muzzle, tip the ears, mane, tail and lower legs.

What is most surprising about the horse is that, physically, it is not ideally suited to many of the tasks it is asked to perform by man. Thus, all riders — whether beginners or experts — cannot be considered complete authorities unless they possess at least a basic knowledge of the physical make-up of the animal they ride.

Such knowledge is essential; at a sale, for instance, the awareness that a good riding horse should have plenty of heart room to give it stamina and toughness may save a buyer from an expensive mistake. On a day-to-day basis, too, knowledge of the so-called points of the horse helps to lessen the risk of injury, particularly where the sensitive joints and muscles are concerned. Such factors should always be born in mind by a rider in his or her approach to the horse and what he or she expects it to do.

The feet

Of all the points of the horse, feet, followed by limbs, come foremost in order of importance; both in the domestic state and in the wild they are the key to the animal's survival. They therefore need to be as correctly conformed as possible — in other words, as perfect as nature will allow.

Well-formed feet are vital, as these have to carry weight and absorb the shock of movement; when a horse jumps, for example, the entire weight of animal and rider falls on one forefoot at the moment of landing. The delicate interior is protected

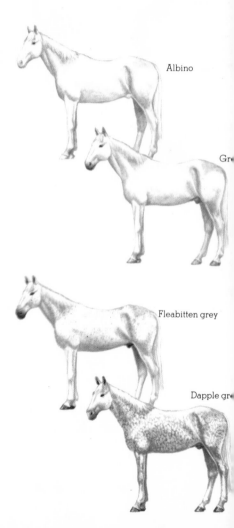

Albino

Gr

Fleabitten grey

Dapple gr

Chestnut

Odd-coloured

Liver chestnut

Strawberry roan

Black

Blue roan

Piebald

Skewbald

Palomino

Bay

Yellow dun

Brown

13

by an outer layer of hoof. This grows at a rate of about 5 mm (0.2 in) per month, so that wear and tear is constantly repaired. Within the foot are the navicular and pedal bones — the end of the pedal being attached to the digital flexor tendon — the digital pad, part of the second phalanx, the corono-pedal joint, cartilages, blood vessels and nerves. The most important of these are the sensitive laminae, which carry food to the hoof and also link it with the bones.

The hoof itself consists of walls, bars, sole and frog. It is particularly important that the frog is sound and well-developed; it acts as an anti-slip device and helps to absorb concussion.

The hindlegs

The hindlegs are the power house of the horse and so are one of its most important features. They are linked to the body by the stifle joint, which, with its patella, functions in a similar manner to the human knee and knee cap. Acting like a pulley block, the patella strengthens the muscles extending the stifle. This, in turn, is controlled by the same ligaments and muscles as the hock, so that the two are synchronized in their movements.

Proceeding down the leg, there follows the gaskin, or second thigh, which runs into the hock. Consisting of a series of joints tightly bound together by ligaments, this is probably the most important part of the leg as it is the main propulsive agent. It articulates directly with the tibia through a single bone — the astralagus.

A good hock is large, flat and almost square when viewed from the side: it is a sign of weakness if the feature looks turned inwards when viewed from the back; the opposite, however, is a sign of strength.

The point of the hock, too, should be we defined, or the strain on the curb ligame will be intensified. Tendons should al stand out clearly, while the lower le should not thicken.

A further feature to look for is sho cannon bones; running from fetlock hock and fetlock to knee, these are anoth sign of strength. The fetlock joint itse should be well-defined and not swolle This leads on to the pastern. This should fairly short and should slope at a gent angle. The more acute the angle, th greater the strain put upon the suspenso tendons and ligaments. However, if th pastern is too short and upright, it cann fulfill its job of absorbing concussion. Th effects of this are then passed directly to th joints — another bad fault.

The foreleg

As the horse has no equivalent to th human collar bone, the foreleg is linked the main part of the body solely by musc and ligamentous tissue. Though th arrangement ensures that a great deal concussion is absorbed, rather than bein passed on to the spine, it also means that th muscles can easily be strained if undu pressure is placed upon them. As consequence, it is particularly important treat all suspected strains promptly.

The foreleg extends from the body belo the point of the shoulder. The forearm ru down into the knee; the former should strong, as a weak forearm means lack muscle. Like the hock, the knee should broad, flat and prominent to take th weight of the body. The cannon, wi clearly-visible tendons, runs down into th fetlock, which is separated from the foot the pastern.

From the front, cannon and forear

White face

Stripe

Blaze

Snip

Star

Facial markings are important means of individual identification. Here, some of the common ones are shown. In the case of a star, the position, as well as size and shape, should be noted; a stripe should be classed as either narrow or broad. A star followed by a stripe is called a disjointed blaze.

White leg markings are also important in identification and should be listed accordingly in, say, a breeding certificate. So, too, should variations in hoof colour. The term stocking (second illustration) is commonly used to describe a patch of white extending over the fetlock; a sock (third illustration) stretches to knee or hock. Other such marks are defined according to their site.

15

The Points of the Horse

The points of the horse.
1 Forelock. **2** Facial crest.
3 Chin groove. **4** Throat.
5 Jugular groove. **6**
Windpipe. **7** Point of
shoulder. **8** Breast. **9** Point
of elbow. **10** Knee. **11**
Cannon. **12** Fetlock. **13**
Pastern. **14** Brisket. **15**
Chestnut. **16** Flexor
tendons. **17** Ergot. **18** Bulb
of heel. **19** Chestnut. **20**
Fetlock. **21** Hoof wall. **22**
Coronet. **23** Shannon
(shank). **24** Hock. **25** Point
of hock. **26** Gaskin. **27**
Hamstring. **28** Sheath. **29**
Flank. **30** Point of buttock.
31 Hip. **32** Hindquarters.
33 Dock. **34** Croup. **35**
Point of croup. **36** Loin.
37 Withers. **38** Crest. **39**
Mane. **40** Atas. **41** Poll.

Knowledge of the points of
the horse is vital for a real
understanding of the
animal. Experts acquire
this by visual examination
and physical touch. By
feeling the point of the
shoulder and other
associated features, for
instance, it is possible for
them to establish what the
actual angle of the
shoulder is and so whether
it is correctly conformed.
An upright shoulder is
often an indication that the
horse lacks physical
endurance. A backward-
sloping shoulder means
that the horse will have a
longer stride and so be
able to cover the ground
more easily.

16

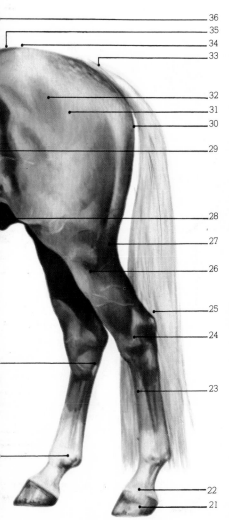

36
35
34
33
32
31
30
29
28
27
26
25
24
23
22
21

should be in a straight line, with the knees evenly placed. Otherwise the knee will be subjected to additional, unwanted strain.

The final feature of the forelegs are the so-called chestnuts — small, horny growths on the inside leg above the knee. These are thought to be vestiges of a former digit and, like fingerprints, each horse's are unique. Their presence is a survival from the distant past.

The body
Running from and supporting the withers — the ridge-like part of the dorsal spine between neck and back — the shoulder should be long and sloping. The greater the slope, the more efficient the shoulder is at absorbing concussion from the forelegs. An upright shoulder can make a horse an uncomfortable ride; endurance, too, can also be reduced, as the length of the stride is considerably shortened.

The breast lies to the front of the chest, between the forelegs. It should be broad and muscular, indicating that there is plenty of heart and lung-room behind it. Narrow-breasted horses invariably lack stamina, while there is the additional problem of trouble with the forelegs if these are set too close together. The neck should be straight and not unduly weighty, since this affects the carriage of the head. On no account should the angle at which the head is set on the neck be too acute, as otherwise the horse's breathing may be restricted.

The size of the head should be in proportion to the total size of the horse; if the head is too big, the forehand will be placed under extra strain. The muzzle should be well-defined, as should the nostrils. Eyes should be large, generous and clear, with uniformly curved lids, while ears should be well-pricked, alert and not over large.

The Points of the Horse

The left side of a mare and the right side of a stallion (below). The mare's complex anatomical make-up includes the following organs: **1** Aorta **2** Left lobe of liver. **3** Stomach. **4** Spleen. **5** Left kidney. **6** Body of uterus. **7** Oesophagus. **8** Trachea. **9** Left vagus nerve. **10** Left ventricle. **11** Left dorsal colon. **12** Small intestine. **13** Left ventral colon. **14** External anal sphincter muscle. **15** Vulva. **16** Urinary bladder. The stallion's include: **1** Right lobe of liver. **2** Right ventricle of heart. **3** Urinary bladder. **4** Rectum. **5** Descending duodenum. **6** Right kidney. **7** Azygos vein. **8** Right testicle. **9** Body of penis. **10** Lateral caecal band. **11** Dorsal sac of caecum. **12** Right ventral colon. **13** Caudal vena cava. Three features make the horse's digestive system unique. The first is that the greatest amount of the alimentary tract — the caesum and colon — is at the rear. The second is the small stomach and the third the lack of a gall bladder.

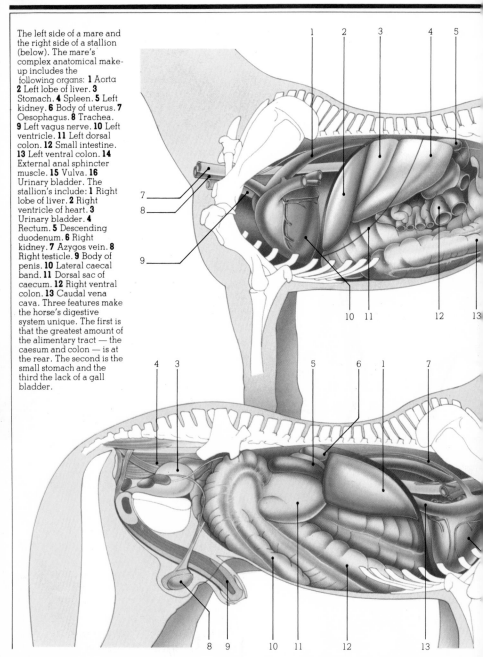

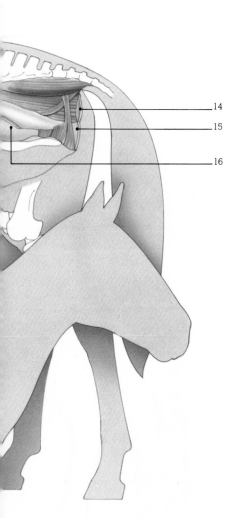

14

15

16

Droopy ears mean that the horse may be sluggish; long ears are often a sign of speed.

Between the ears lies the poll, leading to the top of the neck and the crest, which runs down to the withers and back. In general, the shorter the back, the stronger it will be — this is especially important since the back has to carry the rider's full weight. However, some experts prefer long-backed horses, provided that the horse is what is known as well 'ribbed up'. This means that the distance between the last rib and the point of the hip should not be greater than approximately 50 mm (2 in). The point of the hip itself projects outwards on either side of the backbone above the flanks. This is another possible injury spot, as the projection is relatively unprotected.

Behind the back lies the loin, which extends to the croup, or rump. This leads down to the tail and the dock. The loin should be strong and well-muscled, since it carries the propulsive power to the trunk. It should also be as short as possible, as it is the least supported part of the back. The croup is part of a general feature — the quarters — which also includes, buttock, hip, thigh and stifle. The quarters should be strong and straight, reaching well down into the second thighs. Rounded quarters — technically known as appley quarters — are undesirable.

The flank extends downwards from the lumbar spine. Its most prominent physical feature is at its highest point, just below the loin. This is a triangular indentation called the 'hollow of the flank'. As well as showing through its rise and fall how quickly or slowly the horse is breathing, the condition of the flank also acts as a good guide to the general condition of the horse. If the horse

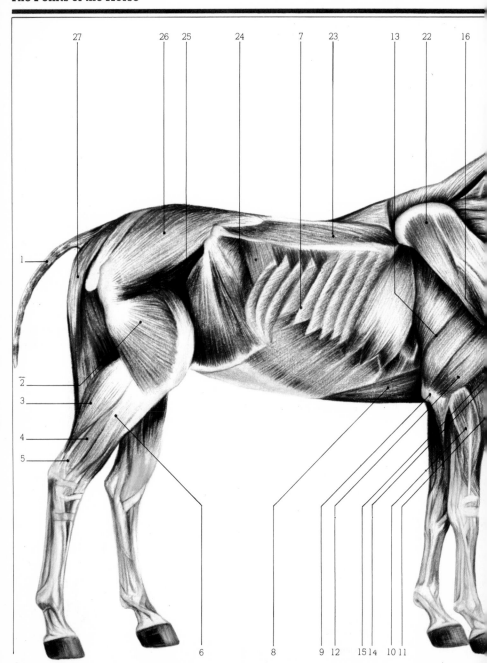

20

19

18

21

is unwell, it will probably be distended or 'tucked up'.

Internal organs

Most of the horse's internal organs work in the same way as those of other mammals, but both the digestive and respiratory systems have features of interest. In the digestive system, in particular, there are three unique features which distinguish the horse from other mammals. These are that the greatest volume of the alimentary tract is at the rear, where the major digestive processes take place; that the stomach is very small for the animal's size; and that there is no gall bladder. The reason for this is probably because the animal needs a constant supply of bile, as it is a continuous feeder.

Three points about the respiratory system are worth noting, since they are connected with the risk of illness or injury.

he principal muscles of he horse. **1** Tail epressors. **2** Lateral astus. **3** Gastrocnemius. **4** ateral digital extensor. **5** eep digital flexor. **6** Long igital extensor. **7** External atercostal. **8** Caudal deep ectoral. **9** Point of elbow. **D** Common digital xtensor. **11** Radial arpal extensor. **12** Lateral ead of triceps. **13** Long ead of triceps. **14** rachialis. **15** Biceps rachii. **16** Teres minor. **17** capular spine. **18** Orbicularis oris. **19** evator muscle of upper p and nostril wing. **20** orrugator supercilii. **21** Iasseter. **22** Supraspinatus. **3** Longissimus dorsi. **24** etractor costae. **25** iacus. **26** Medial gluteal. **7** Semitendinosus.

the outer hindlimb there re the following tendons, s well as muscles. **1**

Achilles tendon. **2** Superficial flexor tendon. **3** Deep flexor tendon. **4** Common digital extensor tendon.

In the outer forelimb: **5** Lateral digital extensor. **6** Superficial flexor tendon. **7** Deep flexor tendon. **8** Common digital extensor tendon. **9** Suspensory ligament. The muscles and tendons of the legs are vital to the horse's survival, but both are prone to injury. Tendons transfer the power produced by muscular contraction to the appropriate bones and joints. They run down the leg; the muscles are grouped together at the top. Each consists of thousands of fibres, lying in connective tissue, surrounded by a smooth membrane and sheath, and lubricated by fluid.

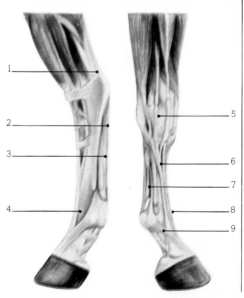

1

2

3

4

5

6

7

8

9

The guttural pouches of the head, for instance, can be infected or become the site of bleeding, while the larynx can become paralyzed on one side. This paralysis obstructs the intake of air and leads to the condition known as roaring. This is particularly noticeable at speed. So, too, is the condition known as broken wind, which is involved with the bronchioles and the alveoli in the lungs.

Teeth and age

The age of a horse is determined by an examination of the six incisor (tearing) teeth in each jaw. In common with other mammals, the horse has two sets of teeth during its life; the first deciduous, or milk, teeth are replaced by permanent teeth as the animal matures, the process usually starting at the age of three and being completed by the age of five. The central teeth erupt first, followed by the laterals and finally by the corners.

The two central incisors are cut when the foal is only four weeks old — they may even be present at birth — and are followed by the laterals and corners at six week and six to nine month intervals respectively. The milk teeth are white, as opposed to the yellow of the permanent teeth, and taper towards the base.

With the complete emergence of the permanent teeth, other considerations have to be taken into account whe[n] determining age. By six, the corne[r] incisors will have worn level; by the age o[f] seven, they will have developed a hoo[k] shape — the 'seven year hook'. Th[is] disappears by the age of eight. At seve[n], too, the dark line known as the dental st[ar] begins to develop; by nine, this is visible o[n] the biting edges of the teeth.

It is now that Galvayne's groove, a long[i]tudinal furrow, appears on the uppe[r] corner incisors near the gum. The grow[th] of this groove serves as one indication o[f] increasing age; another is the increasin[g] slope of the teeth, which reaches its clima[x] between the ages of twenty and twenty-five[.] By the age of fifteen, Galvayne's groov[e] will be halfway down the tooth, while, a[t] twenty, it should have reached the lowe[r] edge. From this time onwards, however, [it] starts to disappear at the same speed as [it] first appeared. By the age of thirty, it w[ill] have vanished completely.

All these points make it possible t[o] determine the age of a horse wit[h] reasonable accuracy. However, after th[is]

Skeletal diagrams show three stages of the gallop (left) and the three stages of jumping (right). Hock and stifle joints play a vital role in both movements. In the gallop, their action gathers up the hind legs a[t] the moment of suspensio[n] while in the jump they power the spring at take-off and gather the hind legs up to clear the obstacle.

ge of eight — when the horse is said to be ged — these methods are not always ertain; this is particularly the case after fteen.

he paces of the horse

he four basic paces of the horse are the valk, trot (jog in Western riding), canter lope in Western riding) and gallop. In ddition, US saddle horses have the extra raits of pace, stepping pace, slow gait and ack.

As officially defined by the International lquestrian Federation (FEI), the walk is a narching pace in which the four legs of the iorse follow each other in four time. The equence of legs is left fore, right hind, ight fore and left hind — two or three legs lways being on the ground. The beats of he pace must be well-accented, even and egular or the walk is considered to be lisunited or broken. The pace itself is sub-livided into medium, collected, extended und free.

The trot is a two-time pace on alternate liagonals (near fore and off hind and vice versa) separated by a moment of uspension. In other words, the diagonal und and forelegs move together, the right oreleg and left hind leg leaving the ground before the left fore and right hind return to t. There are four recognized gaits — vorking, medium, collected and exten-

ded. The rider either rises in the saddle (posts) or remains seated.

Two faults are if the pace is too hurried, so that the forelegs reach the ground before the hinds, or if the hindlegs are dragged. In both cases the result is a four-time pace. A further fault is if one hind leg is brought further forward than the other one.

The canter is a three-time pace, in which the horse bounds forward with either the left or right foreleg leading depending on the direction being taken. In the right canter, for instance, the following sequence must be followed: left hind, left diagonal (right hind and left fore) and right fore. This is followed by a moment of suspension with all four legs in the air before the next stride forwards is taken. The recognized canters are working, medium, collected and extended.

The commonest fault is if the wrong leg leads; in such a case, the canter is termed 'disunited.'

The gallop — the horse's fastest pace — is a four-beat gait. It is a flat-out version of the canter, the chief difference being that the strides and the period of suspension are both much longer. The legs are raised in either of the following sequences — left fore, right fore, left hind and right hind, or the reverse.

A well-trained horse should make the transitions between the various paces

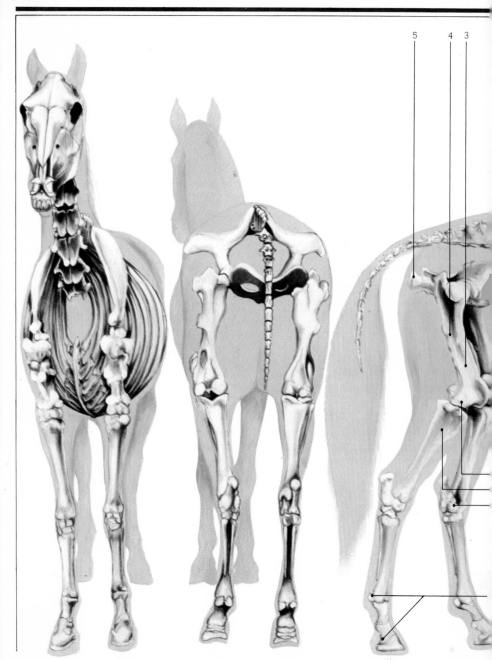

5   4   3

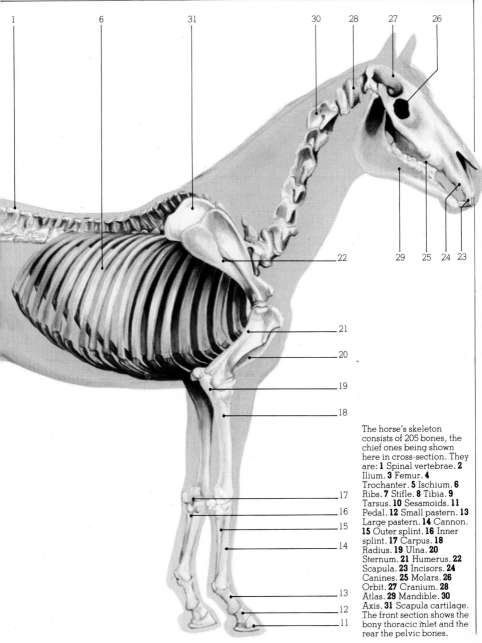

1   6   31   30   28   27   26

22   29   25   24   23

21

20

19

18

17

16

15

14

13

12

11

The horse's skeleton consists of 205 bones, the chief ones being shown here in cross-section. They are: **1** Spinal vertebrae. **2** Ilium. **3** Femur. **4** Trochanter. **5** Ischium. **6** Ribs. **7** Stifle. **8** Tibia. **9** Tarsus. **10** Sesamoids. **11** Pedal. **12** Small pastern. **13** Large pastern. **14** Cannon. **15** Outer splint. **16** Inner splint. **17** Carpus. **18** Radius. **19** Ulna. **20** Sternum. **21** Humerus. **22** Scapula. **23** Incisors. **24** Canines. **25** Molars. **26** Orbit. **27** Cranium. **28** Atlas. **29** Mandible. **30** Axis. **31** Scapula cartilage. The front section shows the bony thoracic inlet and the rear the pelvic bones.

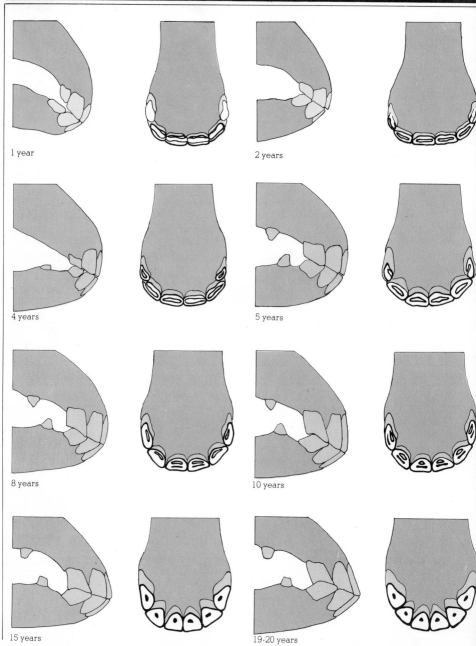

1 year

2 years

4 years

5 years

8 years

10 years

15 years

19-20 years

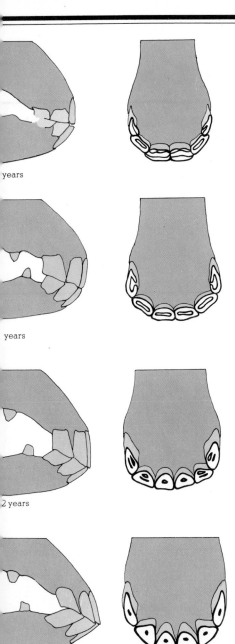

years

years

2 years

20-25 years

quickly and smoothly, not abruptly. The cadence, or rhythm, of the pace should be maintained up to the moment of the change or the halt. The horse should remain calm, light in hand and in the correct position at all times. Bad faults include grinding the teeth and swishing the tail, both being obvious signs of resistance.

Markings and colours

Markings are areas of white on the body, limbs and head of the horse. The terms used to describe them have been officially laid down by the various breeding authorities. On the body these are zebra marks (stripes on the limbs, neck, withers or quarters); and whorls (patterns of hairs around a small central point). Markings on the leg are either socks (white on the fetlock and part of the cannon) or stockings (white stretching from coronet to knee or hock). Socks are always shorter than the stockings.

On the head, markings are a star (a small white patch on the forehead); a stripe (a white line running down the face); a blaze (a broad white line from eyes to muzzle); a

An adult horse has a total of 40 teeth — three incisors, one canine (in colts and geldings) and six cheek teeth (three pre-molars and three molars) on the left and right sides of the upper and lower jaws. The chisel-like front teeth work with the animal's mobile lips when grazing; the back teeth, with their flat top surface criss-crossed with sharp enamel ridges, are ideally suited to grinding the food down.

Horses have two sets of teeth — milk and permanent. These are used to judge the animal's age. Up to five, the gradual emergence of the permanent teeth is the chief guide. At six, the corner incisors have worn level; by seven, they will have developed the 'seven year hook'. At this age, too, the dark dental star begins to develop; by nine it can be seen on the biting edges of the teeth. Simultaneously with this, the longitudinal furrow known as Galvayne's groove starts to emerge on the upper corner incisors. Its growth serves as an indication of age up to twenty; so, too, does the increasing slope of the teeth. However, after fifteen, accuracy is difficult.

27

white face (forehead, eyes, nose and parts of the muzzle); a snip (a small white line running into or around the nostril); and wall eye (blue-white or white colouring in the eye).

Colours of the horse vary widely. They range from bay (brownish horse chestnut, with a black mane, tail and, usually, black lower legs); black (coat, limbs, mane and tail with white points, if any); brown (brown to black points); chestnut (varying shades of red, ranging from dark to liver and light, the last sometimes being termed sorrel); dun (blue or yellow, with black points, dorsal stripe, mane and tail); cream (with light mane and tail and, often, pink eyes); palomino (golden, with flaxen mane and tail); roan (blue or strawberry, the former having black or brown as the basic colour with a touch of white and the latter with chestnut as the base); piebald (black and white); skewbald (red or chestnut or bay and white); pinto (piebald, skewbald or odd-coloured); to grey (white and black on a black skin). This last colour alone has many individual variations — flea-bitten grey and iron grey being two common examples.

Colours and markings are usually listed in any sale document, together with details of type, breeding, age, height and character. The last is a particularly important heading; under it should follow brief descriptions of the mouth, manners, movement and type of ride of the horse concerned. Here it is a good idea to have stated how the horse behaves in traffic — particularly if the intended rider is to be a child.

Measuring height
The height of the horse is measured from the highest point of the withers to the

Walk

Trot

ground. For accuracy, it is important that the animal is standing square on a flat surface.

On the European continent, height is measured in centimetres, while in the UK, Ireland, Australasia and North America it is measured in hands. A hand is officially defined as 10.16 cm (4 in), which is the average distance across a man's knuckles; 15 hands 2 inches, or 15.2 hands, is the accepted way of setting out a fractionalised measurement. The abbreviation *hh* stands for 'hands high'.

Canter

The horse's mind

Leaving aside obvious faults of conformation — many of these are usually present at birth and are often impossible to eliminate fully — few horses are bad. If they are, they have generally been made so by faulty handling, training or inconsiderate riding. In this connection, it is important to realize that, compared to the size of its body, the horse has a small, relatively undeveloped, brain. The animal cannot reason and should not be credited with a human-type intelligence. What the horse does possess is a considerable degree of native instinct and this can be either utilized or marred by man.

Normally, what is required is patience and tact. If a horse shies at the unexpected, punishment will only serve to establish fear in the animal's mind. In the same way, wilfull misbehaviour should always be dealt with immediately — otherwise punishment will not be associated with the crime — while good behaviour should be immediately rewarded.

Gallop

A fit, well-fed, carefully-handled horse, however, will seldom have to face these or indeed any other major problems. It will be a pleasure to ride and to own.

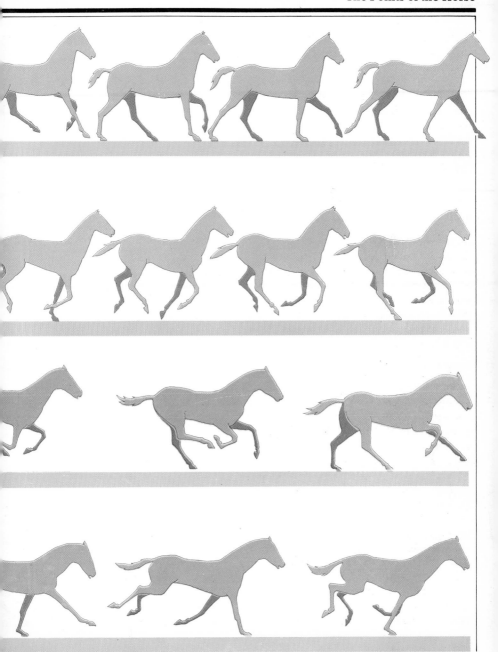

The Breeds of the World

There are literally hundreds of breeds of horse in the world today and their number and composition is constantly changing. There are many reasons for this; a breed can die out because the environment changes, for instance, or because it is no longer useful to man. The latter fate now threatens many of the breeds of heavy horses, whose work is now largely done by machine.

This decline, however, has been partly compensated for by growth in other parts of the horse world. With the great increase in the number of people riding for pleasure in the last twenty years, many countries have started stud books for riding horses to meet the growing demand. These books are divided into two main types. Many are 'open' — that is, the stallion and mare concerned need not be necessarily of the same breed, though they must both be pedigree stock. Others are 'closed'. This means that the offspring can only be registered if the parents are both members of the same breed.

A further means of definition is whether an animal is classed as a hotblood, warmblood, coldblood or pony. Hotbloods are pure-bred, fiery pedigree horses — the English Thoroughbred is a good example. Coldbloods are the heavy horses, the work horses of the world. The warmbloods are lighter animals, usually riding horses, which frequently have both coldblood and warmblood ancestry. Ponies are the small breeds — those which are under 14.2 hands in height — and are the particular favourites of children.

There are, however, certain anomalies within the system. Types, such as Hunter, Hack and Cob, are not registered in the stud books, though a registered Thoroughbred can, of course, be a Hunter. Horses such as the Australian feral Brumby, too, are difficult to place. The Brumby is not a recognized breed — nor is it a type — yet it has been crossbred with domestic stock to produce recognized offspring.

Middle East and Africa

Two of the most influential horses in the world — the Arab and the Barb — originated in these two areas. Though there is some dispute over the Arab's exact origins, the majority opinion is that it first ran wild in the Yemen in the Arabian peninsula. These early horses proved prepotent — that is, they passed their classic qualities of speed, toughness and stamina on from one generation to the next — and today Arab breeding is a world-wide industry. In the Middle East the most important are the Persian and the Egyptian; the former plays an important role in Iran's horse-breeding programme, which also utilizes imported Thoroughbreds and native Turkomans. Most other Iranian strains are covered under one stud book, that of the Plateau Persian. Neighbouring Turkey, too, at one time produced fine Arabs, but a decline in quality meant the importation of the Nonius from Hungary to improve them and breed the Karacabey.

The Barb comes from North Africa. It is

stinguished from the Arab by the fferent appearance of its head, the wer set of its tail and its more fiery mperament. Frequent crossing over e centuries, however, means that few ure-bred Barbs survive today. In South frica, there is only one native horse — e Basuto Pony.

ustralia and East Asia

ustralia's domestic horses are all escended from ones brought to the ountry by the first British settlers in the 790s (the Brumby is descended from ome which escaped to roam wild). The rst major native breed was the Waler, o-called because it was first bred in New outh Wales. Formed by crossing Arab, horoughbred and Anglo-Arab stallions ith local mares and cobs, the breed was e chief source of remounts for the ritish army in India in the nineteenth entury; however, it was not until 1971 at a stud book was finally formed. The nimal was then rechristened the ustralian Stock Horse. The Australian ony's stud book was started in 1929. In ddition to these, many Thoroughbreds, otters and Arabs are bred.

This activity is all part and parcel of ustralia's flourishing horse industry. rom the start, the country proved to be n excellent one for rearing horses, as ew Zealand did later. Today, from riginally having been importers, both ations are now major exporters.

Throughout East Asia, there are many xotic breeds. These include the Indian Manipur (a type rather than a true reed), which was the first polo pony hen the game was taken up by uropeans. China is the home of the ldest surviving breed of horse — the Mongolian Wild Horse, discovered by Colonel Przewalski in 1881 — while among Indonesia's ponies is the romantic Sumba. This is bred as a dancing pony.

The USSR

It was in about 3000 BC that the horse was first domesticated — this momentous event taking place within the boundaries of the present-day USSR. Since that time, horses have played a major role in the region's development. Because of the vast geographic area involved, many different types and breeds have evolved — the Arab having the chief influence in the west and the Mongolian Wild Horse to the east. Today the state authority recognizes forty breeds and breed groups.

Two of the most important of these are the Akhal Teké and the Orlov Trotter. The Akhal Teké is descended from the ancient Turkoman horses and is noted for its powers of endurance. The Orlov Trotter is of more recent origin. It was first bred in 1877 by Count Orlov by crossing an Arab stallion with a Dutch/Danish mare. The product was later refined to produce the Russian Trotter.

This process of refinement is now official breeding policy and is carried out by crossing existing stock with outside breeds. The Don, for example, has had Thoroughbred and Arab blood added; it itself was used to toughen other breeds.

In addition, new breeds have been developed, while, at the same time, some of the celebrated nineteenth-century breeds have been allowed to die out — though not before being used as foundation stock for their replacements. Thus the Strelets (a large Arab) was used as a basis for the Tersky (established 1948), and the Klepper (a tough preponent pony) for the Toric and Viatka.

Eastern Europe

Out of all the countries in Europe, Poland has the largest horse population; today it stands at about 3 million. Over the centuries, many different types of horse have been bred for a variety of uses, but a constant factor has been the influence of Arab blood. The Wielkopolski, for instance, has Arab, Thoroughbred and Trakehner ancestry. It is one of the many products of the state studs, whose other successes include the world-famous Polish Arab.

The oldest surviving native pony is the Tarpan, whose origins go back to the Ice Age. However, the modern Tarpan is an act of skillful recreation. Its influence is also seen in the Huçul and the Konik, the latter being the foundation stock for many other breeds.

Hungary's horse-breeding history, too, shows Arab influence. The tough horses of the early Magyars were later cross-bred with Arabs to produce many famous types, the most celebrated being the Shagya. This, in turn, played a vital part in the foundation of the Lipizzaner. Other major influences were the British Thoroughbreds which were used in the founding of the Furioso strain. A French stallion produced the Nonius.

Czechoslovakia and Bulgaria are also important horse centres. The former has the oldest operational stud in the world at Kladruby, where the white Kladrubers are bred. Bulgaria produces three well-known half-breds — the Pleven, the Danubian and the East Bulgarian — while Yugoslavia's most important native

product is the Bosnian Pony.

Scandinavia

The demands of war played a part in th development of two of Denmark's bes known horses. The Jutland — today work horse — carried many mediev knights into battle; the Frederiksborç bred from a mixture of Andalusia Neapolitan, Arab and British blood in th sixteenth century, similarly served as charger.

Other Danish horses are the Fjor Pony and a relatively recent innovatio the Danish Sports Horse.

Sweden has the Swedish Halfbred — good dressage and eventing horse — th Swedish Ardennes as a work horse an the Gotland as its native pony. Th Norwegian pony is the Norwegian Fjor while the country also produces the Dø and the Døle Trotter. Finland has th Finnish Horse and Iceland the Iceland Pony.

Switzerland, Austria, Belgiur Holland

The most celebrated Austrian horse without question the Lipizzaner, th world-famous mounts used by th Spanish Riding School in Vienna Spanish blood, too, played a major pa in the founding of the breed; it was fir bred at the stud founded by the Archduk Charles in 1580 at Lipizza near Trieste The horse's present breeding centre is Piber in south Austria.

The other noted Austrian horses ar the Halflinger and the Noriker. The latte was originally bred by the Roman Home-produced half-breds, Hanoveriar and Trakeheners are used to breed th Austrian Riding Horse.

The Belgian, together with the Ardennes, are Belgium's chief work horses. The former is a direct descendant of the medieval Flanders Horse. The Belgium Warmblood is a more recent innovation. Neighbouring Holland has three native breeds — the Gelderland, the Gronigen and the Friesland — as well as stud books for Arabs, Hackneys, Dutch Warmbloods, Trotters, Racehorses and five pony breeds.

Switzerland's two historic horses are the Einsielder and the Freiberger. Since the 1960s, they have been joined by the Swiss Halfbred.

West and East Germany

West Germany is particularly noted for its fine riding horses, the best known of which are the Hanoverian, the Trakehner and the Holstein. The Hanoverian owes a great deal of its success to the English Thoroughbred blood introduced between 1714 and 1837. Its great rival, the Trakehner, had its original home in East Prussia, where the founding stud was established in 1732. In 1944, however, the advancing Soviet armies forced evacuation; 700 mares and a handful of stallions reached the west to form the nucleus of the present breed. The Holstein, for its part, has been bred in Schleswig-Holstein since the fourteenth century.

All other German warmbloods have used these three breeds as foundation stock, with other blood being added if necessary. German's heavy horses, the Rhineland and the Schleswig Heavy Draught, similarly owe a debt to imported stock.

East Germany's two leading breeds are the Mecklenburg and the East Frisian; they are closely related to the Hanoverian and the Oldenburg respectively.

France

More than in any other Western country, the state dominates horse-breeding in France through the Service des Havas, which is responsible for the industry. The Service runs twenty-three stallion depots, which, in the best breeding areas, such as Normandy, house as many as 200 stallions.

The main competition horse is the Selle Francais, an amalgamation of forty-five different breed groups founded in 1965. Of these, the Anglo-Norman and Anglo-Arab were the most influential — Arabs, indeed, are the ancestors of all French breeds and are still extensively used for cross-breeding.

French Thoroughbreds and Trotters are world-famous, while the Percheron is the best-known heavy horse. Ponies include the Camargue, the Basque and the Landais.

Southern Europe

Italy's most famous horse was the medieval Neapolitan, which found its way into the royal courts of Europe as a high school horse and also became the foundation stock for many breeds. So, too, did the Andalusian, the most important of the horses of Spain. Nowadays, however, imported breeds dominate the Italian scene and native riding horses, such as the Murghese and Calabrese, are on the decline.

Portugal's breeds — the Altér-Real and the Lusitano — have close links with the Andalusian, as they have similar Arab and Barb ancestry. So, too, has the Minho pony; the other native Portuguese breed is the tough Sorraia. Greece's native stock consists of three ponies — the Peneia, Pindos and Skyros.

South America

The Criollo, the horse of the Argentinian *gaucho* (cowboy) is descended from a group of Andalusian horses brought by the Spanish to the New World, which escaped to roam wild. The Argentinian polo pony is a cross between it and the Thoroughbred, while Brazil's Crioulo is a smaller version of the Criollo. Other Brazilian horses of note are the Mangalarga and the Campolino, the latter being selectively bred from the former. Peru's Steeping Horse, with its unique lateral gait, gave rise to Puerto Rico's Paso Fino. Venezuela, like most South American countries, has its own version of the Criollo — the Llanero.

North America

Though North America was the original home of *Equus caballos,* horses died out there at the end of the Ice Age — not to reappear until the Spanish landed there in 1511. Some of these escaped to give the Indians their Mustangs, but the only Indian horse to be recognized as a breed is the Appaloosa. This was first bred by the Nez Perce tribe at the end of the eighteenth century.

Later colonists also brought horses with them and it was from these that the first native breeds emerged. The earliest of these was the Narrangansett Pacer; it was followed by the Quarter Horse, the oldest surviving US breed. Its name comes from the test of quality instituted by its Virginian breeders — racing it over a quarter of a mile. An all-purpose

animal, it proved suited to many tasks, chief amongst these being its use as a cow pony. It is also used in rodeos, for riding, racing and in shows. Another old established US breed is the Morgan, so called because its founding sire was owned by an inn keeper, Justin Morgan.

With the Thoroughbred and the Narrangansett Pacer, the Morgan was also the foundation stock for the Saddlebred, a spectacular horse with three or five smooth gaits. The Tennessee Walking Horse, officially recognized in 1935, has even smoother paces.

In more recent times, the US has defined breeds that do not, as yet, breed true on the basis of colour. One such breed is the Palomino; others are the Indian Pinto and the Albino. The US native pony is the Pony of the Americas, developed in the 1960s. Imported horses, particularly Thoroughbreds, also play an extremely important role on the American scene.

Canada has no native horse breed, the Canadian Cutting Horse being defined as a type.

Britain and Ireland

Britain and Ireland have bred some of the finest horses in the world. The UK's greatest contribution has been the Thoroughbred, the world's fastest and most valuable breed whose origins date back to the seventeenth and eighteenth centuries. Starting from around 1660, more than 200 Arab-type horses were imported to improve the native British racing stock. It is still uncertain whether these imported horses were crossed with native racing mares — the now extinct Galloway ponies — or whether the foundations were purely Oriental. There is no question, however, that the three

reatest influences were the stallions
arley Arabian, Byerley Turk and
Godolphin Barb. The first was the
riginator of the Blandford, Phalaris,
Gainsborough, Son in Law and St Simon
nes, the second of the Herod line and
e third of the Matcham line.

Arab blood, too, has played an impor-
nt part in the development of the Welsh
ountain Pony, which is officially
escribed as 'an Arab in miniature'.
imilarly, the eye-catching Hackney
orse, with its spectacular high-stepping
ot, combines Yorkshire Hackney and
rab blood. There are also traces of the
ow extinct Norfolk Trotter in its
ncestry.

The UK's other main contribution to
e horse world has been its native
onies. These have a long history, dating
ack to the original wild stock that
amed moor, forest and fell.

Nine native breeds of pony now exist,
f which the Exmoor is probably the
ldest. Its presence is recorded in the
omesday Book, but its origins go back
ir further − to prehistoric times when
e remote ancestors of the Exmoors
rossed the land bridge that then linked
ritain and the Continent. Its neighbour,
e Dartmoor, is bigger and not as pure
red. Further to the east, the New Forst
ony has had additions of Arab,
horoughbred and Galloway blood.
mong the doners of Arabs was Queen
ictoria, who in 1852 lent a stallion to
nprove the breed. This ran wild with the
ares for eight years and was followed by
vo more − also donated by the Queen −
1 1885. The result was a well
roportioned, sure footed riding pony,
tanding about 14 hh, with an easy action
nd a good temperament.

The Pennines are the home of the Fell
Pony; its neighbour to the east — the Dale
— is the largest of Britain's native pony
breeds. Across the border in Scotland,
the Highland shares a common ancestry
with the Fell and the Dale. However,
additions of Arab and French blood have
led to the emergence of two quite distinct
varieties — the Highland Pony and the
Highland Garron. The latter is bigger
and stronger than the former.

Even further to the north lies the island
home of the Shetland Pony. The ancestry
of the small but sturdy breed dates back
to around 500 BC, when ponies were
introduced to the Shetlands from
Scandinavia. Subsequently, these
ponies were probably crossed with
animals brought from the mainland by
the Celts.

The only recognized British riding/
driving horse is the Cleveland Bay,
which has been bred in Yorkshire for over
two hundred years. The largest British
horse is the Shire, which is probably a
descendant of the medieval Great Horse.
So, too, is the Scottish Clydesdale. The
slightly smaller Suffolk Punch originated
in the 1760s.

Ireland's horse industry plays a major
part in the country's economic life and
many of the horses bred there become
world-beaters, particularly in the racing
field. On the west coast, the tough,
handsome Connemara Pony still roams
wild, as it has done for centuries. In
origin, it probably has the same ancestry
as the Highland; the chief difference lies
in the injection of Spanish blood the
Connemara received from the horses and
ponies that swam ashore after the
shipwreck of the Spanish Armada in
1588.

Akhal Teké

Akhal Teké

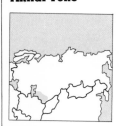

Warmblood
Origin Turkoman Steppes.
Height 15 hands.
Colour bay, chestnut, grey
or black, usually with
metallic sheen.
Physique elegant, long
head, straight profile,
long, thin neck, long back,
low-set silky tail, long legs
with light, strong bone.
Features hardy,
temperamental, fast and
versatile.
Temperament bold, but
can be obstinate.
Use riding.

Albino

Warmblood
Origin USA.
Height any.
Colour white with pink
skin, pale blue or dark
brown eyes.
Physique lightweight
frame, otherwise varies.
Temperament kindly,
intelligent.
Use riding.

Altér Real

Altér Real

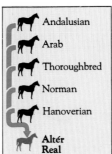

Andalusian

Arab

Thoroughbred

Norman

Hanoverian

Altér Real

Warmblood
Origin Alentejo province,
Portugal.
Height 15.2 hands.
Colour chestnut, bay or
piebald.
Physique smallish head
with straight profile, short,
arched neck, close-

coupled, strong loins and
hindquarters and good,
fine bone.
Features extravagant high
knee action.
Temperament intelligent,

highly-strung, brave.
Use riding, especially
high school equitation.

Andalusian

Andalusian

Warmblood
Origin Andalusia.
Height 16 hands.
Physique largish head, almost convex profile, strong, arched neck, deep, short-coupled body round hindquarters and short cannon bones.

Features athletic, great presence, an elegant, springy action.
Temperament intelligent, affectionate.
Use high school equitation, general riding.

Garrano

Noriker

Barb

Arab

Andalusian

Anglo-Arab

Anglo-Arab

Warmblood
Origin Britain, France and
Poland.
Height 16 hands.
Colour solid colours.
Physique good shoulder
and well-proportioned,
powerful hindquarters.
Features stamina and
good movement.
Temperament brave,
sweet-tempered, intelligent.
Use riding, competitions
and racing.

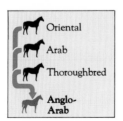

Appaloosa

Appaloosa

Warmblood
Origin western USA.
Height 15 hands.
Colour six basic patterns
of spots usually on roan or
white, white sclera around
eye.
Physique short-coupled
thin mane and tail, hard

feet which are often
striped.
Features striking
appearance.
Temperament tractable,
hardy with great
endurance.
Use as a cow pony, a
pleasure and parade horse
and in the circus.

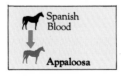

Spanish
Blood

Appaloosa

Arab

Arab

horoughbred.
rigin Arabia.
eight 14.3 hands.
olour bay, chestnut,
rey.

hysique small, tapering
ead, concave face, broad
rehead, large, dark
yes, small ears, arched

neck, long, sloping
shoulder, short straight
back, straight croup, high-
set tail, fine legs but very
hard bone.
Features fast free-floating
action, stamina and
toughness.
Temperament spirited,
enduring intelligent, bold.
Use improving other
breeds, long distance and
general riding.

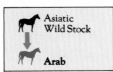

Asiatic
Wild Stock

Arab

Ardennais

Ardennais

Coldblood
Origin France — Lorraine Champagne, foothills of Vosges.
Height 15.3 — 16 hands.
Colour bay, chestnut or roan.
Physique short, stocky compact, heavyweight, with a large bone structure, strong head and broad face.
Features hardy.
Temperament docile, gentle and willing.
Use agriculture.

Ardennes

Coldblood
Origin Belgium — the Ardennes.
Height 15.3 hands
Colour bay, chestnut or roan.
Physique muscular, short-coupled body, crested neck, broad chest and short, feathered legs.
Features strong, active.

Great War Horse

Belgian

Oriental

Ardennes

Temperament gentle an willing.
Use agriculture.

Australian Pony

Pony.
Origin Australia.
Height 13 hands.
Colour most colours.
Physique Arab head,

Australian Stock Horse

ngish neck, sloping
houlder, deep girth,
und hindquarters.
emperament intelligent
nduring, courageous.
se riding.

Arab

Welsh
Pony

Exmoor
Pony

Shetland
Pony

Thoroughbred

**Australian
Pony**

Australian Stock Horse

Warmblood.
Origin New South Wales.
Height 16 hands.
Colour all colours.
Physique varies, usually
alert head, deep girth,
strong back.
Features hardy, with a

strong constitution.
Temperament reliable,
versatile, hard working.
Use herding and cavalry.

Avelignese

Pony.
Origin the Italian Alps and
Appennines.

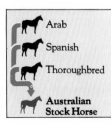

Arab

Spanish

Thoroughbred

**Australian
Stock Horse**

Height 14 hands.
Colour chestnut with
flaxen mane and tail.
Physique heavy-frame,
short, feathered legs and
large, hard feet.
Features sure-footed and
long-lived.
Temperament good-
tempered, gentle, easy-to-
train and tough.
Use pack work in the
mountains, light
agricultural work.

Oriental

Halflinger

Avelignese

Barb

Balearic

Pony.
Origin Majorca.
Height about 14 hands.
Colour bay or brown.
Physique fine head,
usually Roman nose, light,
tough frame and hard feet.
Features free, graceful
action.

Temperament good,
docile and patient.
Use agricultural work and
driving.

Bali

Pony.
Origin Indonesia/Bali.
Height 12.2 hands.
Colour dun with dorsal.
stripe and dark points.
Physique sturdy frame.
Features frugal and
strong.
Temperament good
workhorse.
Use riding and general
pack work.

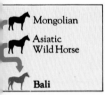

Barb

Warmblood.
Origin Algeria and
Morocco.
Height 14.2 hands.
Colour bay, brown,
chestnut, black and grey.
Physique long head,
straight profile, sloping
quarters, low-set tail and
long, strong legs.
Features frugal and
tough.
Temperament docile and
courageous.

Use adding strength to
other breeds, such as the
Andalusian and
Thoroughbred, riding and
transport.

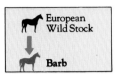

Bashkirsky

Pony.
Origin Bashkiria, USSR.
Height 13.2 hands.
Colour bay, dun or
chestnut.
Physique thickset,
prominent wither, longish
back, low-set tail and short
legs.
Features tough.
Temperament calm,
good-tempered and hardy.
Use riding and pulling
sleighs; mares are milked
for *kumiss*.

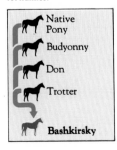

Basque

Pony.
Origin Basque region of
France.
Height 13 hands.
Colour most.
Physique primitive, with
head slightly concave,
small ears, short neck and
long back.
Features stamina and
toughness.
Temperament quick to
mature and enduring.
Use mining, riding.

Basuto

Basuto

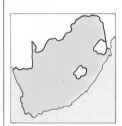

Pony.
Origin South Africa.
Height 14.2 hands.
Colour chestnut, bay, brown and grey.
Physique quality head, longish neck and back, strong, straightish shoulder, short legs and hard hooves.
Features sure-footed and tough, with great stamina.
Temperament fearless and self-reliant.
Use racing, polo and riding.

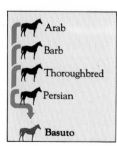

Arab
Barb
Thoroughbred
Persian

Basuto

Batak

Pony.
Origin Sumatra, Indonesia.
Height 12.2 hands.
Colour most colours.
Physique comparatively refined, good conformation.
Features frugal.
Temperament spirited, good-tempered, handles well.
Use agriculture and transport.

Native Pony
Arab

Batak

Belgian Heavy Draught

avarian

armblood.
igin Lower Bavaria,
est Germany.
eight 16 hands.
lour solid colours.
ysique medium-sized
me, deep girth and
oad chest.
atures derived from

Rottaler war horse.
Temperament sensible,
docile and willing.
Use riding.

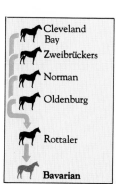

Cleveland
Bay

Zweibrückers

Norman

Oldenburg

Rottaler

Bavarian

Belgian Heavy Draught

(Brabant)
Coldblood.
Origin Brabant.
Height 16.2 hands.
Colour red roan with black
points, or chestnut.
Physique heavy, large

frame, shortish back, short
legs with feather on
fetlocks.
Features strength,
presence and good action.
Temperament courageous
and tractable.
Use draught work.

Flanders
Horse

Ardennes

Ancient
Forest Horse

Belgian

Bosnian

Bhutia

Pony.
Origin India.
Height 12 hands.
Colour grey.
Physique thickset and
short-coupled.
Features sure-footed and
tough.

Temperament alert and
intelligent, but not always
good-tempered.
Use transportation in the
mountains.

Mongolian
Pony

**Spiti
Bhutia**

Bosnian

Pony.
Origin Yugoslavia.
Height 12.2. hands.
Colour dun, brown, grey,
black or chestnut.
Physique compact
mountain pony.
Features endurance.

Temperament tough,
affectionate and very
intelligent.
Use agricultural work.

Tarpan

Oriental

Steppe
Pony

Bosnian

Breton

oulonnais

oldblood.
rigin Northern France.
eight 16.1 hands.
olour grey, chestnut or
ay.
hysique similar to
ercheron, silky coat.
eatures lively and active.

Temperament good
tempered, intelligent.
Use draught.

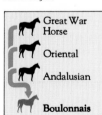

Great War
Horse

Oriental

Andalusian

Boulonnais

Breton
Coldblood.
Origin France.
Height 16.1 hands.
Colour grey, chestnut or
bay.
Physique Postier Breton;

close coupled, elegant
head and short legs with
little feather. Draught
Breton; larger, more
elongated body.
Features strong and
active, although the
Draught is less energetic.
Temperament sweet
tempered, lively and
willing.
Use agricultural work.

Draught
Breton
Norfolk
Trotter

Hackney

**Postier
Breton**

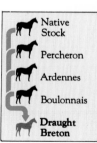

Native
Stock

Percheron

Ardennes

Boulonnais

**Draught
Breton**

51

Budyonny

Budyonny
(Budenny)

Warmblood.
Origin USSR.
Height 15.3 hands.
Colour chestnut or bay
with golden sheen.
Physique strong frame,
crested neck, close-
coupled and deep bodied.
Features fast and
enduring.
Temperament intelligent;
calm and energetic.
Use riding, competitions
and steeplechasing.

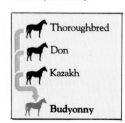

Thoroughbred

Don

Kazakh

Budyonny

Burma

urma

Use polo and general.

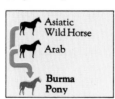

Asiatic
Wild Horse

Arab

**Burma
Pony**

ony.
rigin Burma.
eight 13 hands.
olour all colours.
hysique thickset with
gh-set tail.

eatures strong hill-pony.
emperament active, but
an be slow in response.

Calabrese

Warmblood.
Origin Calabria, Italy.
Height about 16 hands.
Colour solid colours.
Physique middleweight,
short-coupled riding
horse.
Features handsome saddle
horse.

Temperament intelligent,
easy to manage.
Use riding.

Neapolitan

Calabrese

Camargue

Camargue
(Camarguais)

Pony.
Origin The Camargue, Rhone delta, France.
Height 14 hands.
Colour grey.
Physique Oriental-type head, straightish shoulder, short body, fine legs with hard bone.
Features hardy.
Temperament quiet and reliable when broken.
Use herding, trekking, also roams wild.

Campolino

Warmblood.
Origin Brazil.
Height 14.3-15 hands.
Physique similar to the Mangalarga, but with a heavier frame and more bone.
Features hardy dual-purpose horse.
Temperament tough, willing and enduring.
Use riding and light draught work.

Canadian Cutting Horse

Canadian Cutting Horse

Features fast and agile.
Temperament quick
witted and intelligent.
Use competition and stock
work.

Warmblood.
Origin North America.
Height 15.2-16.1 hands.
Colour almost any colour.
Physique like the US
Quarter Horse, with long
body, short legs, powerful
hindquarters.

55

Caspian

Caspian Pony

Pony.
Origin Iran.
Height 10-11.2 hands.
Colour grey, brown, bay
or chestnut.
Physique Arab-type head,
fine boned.
Features sure-footed.

Temperament gentle,
tractable and intelligent,
ideal for children.
Use transport and riding.

Cleveland Bay

Cleveland Bay

Warmblood.
Origin Yorkshire.
UK.
Height 16 hands.
Colour bay or brown;
white markings not
desirable.
Physique large head,
convex profile, longish

back, high-set tail and
good bone.
Features versatile, strong
and long-lived.
Temperament intelligent,
calm and sensible.
Use riding and driving.

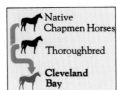

Native
Chapmen Horses

Thoroughbred

Cleveland
Bay

Clydesdale

Coldblood.
Origin Lanarkshire, UK.
Height 16.2 hands.
Colour dark with white on
face and legs.
Physique long, crested
neck high withers,
straightish hind legs,
much feather.

Features active.
Temperament brave and
friendly.
Use draught.

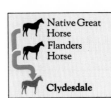

Native Great
Horse

Flanders
Horse

Clydesdale

57

Connemara

Comtois

Coldblood.
Origin Franche Comté, France.
Height 15.1 hands.
Colour bay or chestnut.
Physique largish head, straight neck, long, straight back and little feather.

Features active and sure footed.
Temperament courageous, kind and willing.
Use agriculture.

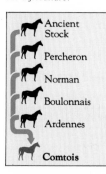

Ancient Stock

Percheron

Norman

Boulonnais

Ardennes

Comtois

Connemara

Pony.
Origin County Connaught, Eire.
Height 13.2 hands.
Colour grey.
Physique compact, intelligent head, crested neck, sloping shoulder and deep, strong, sloping

hindquarters.
Features sure-footed, hardy; a good jumper.
Temperament intelligent tractable and kind, good with children.
Use riding and driving.

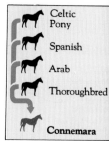

Celtic Pony

Spanish

Arab

Thoroughbred

Connemara

Criollo

Criollo

Warmblood.
Origin Argentina.
Height 14.2 hands.
Colour dun with dark points, dorsal stripe with dark snippets; red and blue roan, sorrel and skewbald.
Physique short head tapering to muzzle, short-coupled, sturdy frame, strong, sloping shoulder, short legs, good bone and small, hard feet.
Features tough and manoeuvrable.
Temperament willing, tough and enduring.
Use long-distance riding and ranch work.

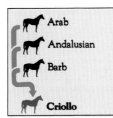

Crioulo

Warmblood.
Origin Brazil.
Height 15 hands.
Colour lighter Criollo colours.
Physique prominent withers, high-set tail and longish neck.
Features frugal and tough.
Temperament enduring.
Use riding and herding.

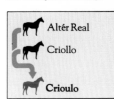

59

Dale

Dale

Pony.
Origin Eastern Pennines, UK.
Height 14.1 hands.
Colour dark colours, with no white except star.
Physique powerful frame, straightish shoulder, fine hair on heels and thick mane and tail.
Features strong (can pull one ton), sure-footed.
Temperament sensible, quiet and hard working.
Use pack, agricultural work and riding.

Celtic Pony

Galloway

Friesian

Welsh Cob

Dale

Danish Sport Horse

Warmblood.
Origin Denmark.
Height 16.1 hands.
Colour all colours.
Physique varies, middleweight build.
Features good general riding and competition horse.
Temperament versatile, competitive.
Use general riding.

Hanoverian

Native Halfbred

Thoroughbred

Trakehner

Polish

Anglo-Norman

Danish Sports Horse

Dartmoor

ᴀnubian

Temperament active and docile.
Use light draught, riding and competitions.

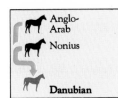

...rmblood.
...**gin** Bulgaria.
...**ght** 15.2 hands.
...**lour** dark chestnut or ...ck.
...**ysique** short-coupled, ...p girth, high-set tail ...d fine strong legs.
...**atures** strength.

Dartmoor

Pony
Origin Dartmoor, Devon, UK.
Height 12.1 hands.
Colour bay, black or brown.
Physique small head, strong shoulders, back and loins, high-set tail and full mane and tail.
Features long-lived, sure-footed and tough.
Temperament kind and sensible, ideal for children.
Use riding.

Døle

Døle

Warmblood.
Origin Norway.
Height 15 hands.
Colour black, brown or bay.
Physique two types; heavy draught — similar to the UK Dale; pony type — upright shoulder, deep girth, short legs with good bone and little feather.
Features tough, versatile.
Temperament active and patient, adaptable.
Use agricultural work, riding and driving.

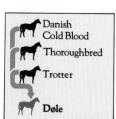

Døle Trotter

Warmblood.
Origin Norway.
Height 15 hands.
Colour black, brown or bay.
Physique lighter version of Dole with no feather.
Features good trotting horse.
Temperament active, tough and competitive.
Use trotting races.

Don

Warmblood.
Origin Central Asia (steppes).
Height 15.2 hands.
Colour chestnut, bay or grey.

Don

Physique deep body,
[lo]ng, straight neck and
[ba]ck, long legs.
Features versatile, frugal,
[wi]th great stamina.
Temperament energetic,
[ca]lm and reliable.
[U]se the original Cossack
[ho]rse, now used for
[dr]iving, riding and long
[di]stance racing.

Oriental
Thoroughbred
Orlov Trotter
Turkoman
Karabakh
Karabair
Don

Dulmen

Pony.
Origin Westphalia.

Height 12.3 hands.
Colour black, brown or dun.
Physique various.
Features semi-wild breed.
Temperament hardy.
Use riding.

Dutch Draught

Cold blood.
Origin Holland.

Height 16.1 hands.
Colour bay, chestnut or
black.
Physique tall with a
powerful front and deep,
strong body.
Features strength and
stamina.
Temperament kind but
spirited, hard-working.
Use draught.

East Friesian

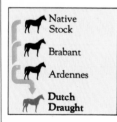

Native Stock

Brabant

Ardennes

Dutch Draught

East Bulgarian

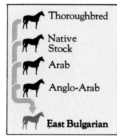

Thoroughbred

Native Stock

Arab

Anglo-Arab

East Bulgarian

Warmblood.
Origin Bulgaria.
Height 15.3 hands.
Colour chestnut or black.
Physique smallish head, straight profile, deep girth and longish, straight back.
Features energetic,

hardy, fast.
Temperament active, intelligent, good-tempered.
Use riding, agriculture, competitions and steeple chasing.

East Friesian

Warmblood.

Origin East Germany.
Height 16.1 hands.
Colour solid colours.
Physique similar to the Oldenburg but lighter, with a more elegant head.
Features quality saddle and carriage horse.
Temperament bold, kind and spirited.
Use riding and light draught work.

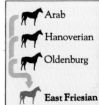

Arab

Hanoverian

Oldenburg

East Friesian

Exmoor

Egyptian Arab

...oroughbred.
...gin Egypt..
...ght 14.3 hands.
...our grey.
...sique two types; the
...aylan is more rangey
...the short-coupled
...avy.
...tures speed.

Temperament spirited
and courageous, tough.
Use racing, breeding,
general riding.

Einsiedler

Warmblood.
Origin Switzerland.
Height 16 hands.
Colour bay or chestnut.
Physique well-

proportioned, strong
frame.
Features free action,
energetic.
Temperament bold,
intelligent, tractable and
versatile.
Use riding and driving.

Ancient Stock
Hackney
Anglo-Norman
Einsiedler

Exmoor

Pony.
Origin Exmoor, Somerset
and Devon, UK.
Height 12 hands.
Colour bay, brown or dun
with black points, light
mealy muzzle, no white.
Physique prominent 'toad'
eyes, wide chest, strong

Falabella

quarters and thick,
springy coat with no bloom
in winter.
Features, strength and
endurance.
Temperament intelligent,
semi-wild, but good for
children if well-trained.
Use riding.

Falabella

Pony.
Origin Argentina.
Height 7 hands.
Colour all colours.
Physique the smallest
pony in the world.
Features hardy and full of
character.
Temperament friendly

and intelligent, an ideal
pet.
Use harness pony and pet.

Finnish

ny.
igin Cumbria, UK.
ight 13.2 hands.
lour black, brown or
y.
ysique great substance,
nimum 8 inches of bone,
e hair on heels and
ng, curly mane and tail.

Features strength and stamina; a fast trotter.
Temperament lively and alert, a good worker.
Use all-purpose, driving agricultural work, pack and trekking.

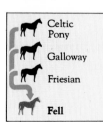

Celtic Pony

Galloway

Friesian

Fell

Finnish

Coldblood.
Origin Finland.
Height 15.2 hands.
Colour chestnut, bay and brown.
Physique short neck, upright shoulder, deep, strong legs, light feather.
Features tough, long-

lived, fast.
Temperament even-tempered, kind, gentle and quiet, yet lively and willing.
Use timber hauling, agriculture and trotting.

Indigenous Forest pony

Finnish Draught

Finnish

Finnish Universal

Fjord

Fjord

Pony.
Origin Norway.
Height 14 hands.
Colour dun, cream or
yellow with dorsal stripe
and upright black and
silver mane.
Physique small head,
strong, short neck and

powerful, compact body.
Features sure-footed, very
hardy.
Temperament gentle and
strong-willed, hard
working and tireless.
Use mountain work,
agriculture, transport,
riding and driving.

Franches Montagnes

Franches Montagnes
(Freiberger)

Warmblood
Origin Avenche,
Switzerland.
Height 15.1 hands.
Colour blue roan or grey;
solid colours.

Physique powerful,
compact frame.
Features stamina,
strength.
Temperament active,
versatile and hard
working.
Use agricultural work.

Freiberger
Cold Blood
Shagya
Arab
**Franches
Montagnes**

Fredericksborg

Fredericksborg

good-tempered and
willing.
Use light draught, riding.

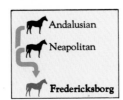

Warmblood.
Origin Denmark.
Height 15.3 hands.
Colour chestnut.
Physique strong, plain
harness horse, large chest,
strong back.
Features active.
Temperament tractable,

French Trotter

rench Trotter

Features athletic and fast.
Temperament tough,
willing and competitive.
Use trotting, riding and
cross-breeding.

Norfolk
Trotter
Anglo-
Norman
**French
Trotter**

armblood
rigin Calvados.
eight 16.1 hands.
olour any solid colour.
hysique tall, light-
amed horse with a fine
ead, prominent wither,
rong back and sloping
ndquarters.

Friesian

Friesian

Warmblood
Origin Holland.
Height 15 hands.
Colour black.
Physique longish head,
crested neck, round
hindquarters, good bone,
feather and full mane and
tail.

Features great presence.
Temperament willing,
good-tempered, hard-
working.
Use circus, riding and
driving, and all-round
work horse.

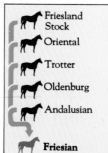

Friesland
Stock

Oriental

Trotter

Oldenburg

Andalusian

Friesian

Furioso

Furioso

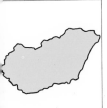

Warmblood
Origin Hungary.
Height 16 hands.
Colour dark colours.
Physique muscular body, straightish back, sloping hindquarters and low-set tail.
Features robust.

Temperament active, intelligent, tractable.
Use riding, competitions driving and steeple-chasing.

English Halfbred

Arab

Thoroughbred

Furioso

Galiceno

Galiceno

intelligent, versatile, brave and gentle.
Use ranch work and transportation.

Pony
Origin Mexico.
Height 12.2. hands.
Colour bay, black or dun.
Physique short-coupled, narrow frame.
Features versatile, natural running walk.
Temperament very

Garrano (Minho)

Features strong and sure footed.
Temperament hardy, quick, good-tempered.
Use riding and pack.

Pony
Origin Garranho do Minho, Traz dos Montes, Portugal.
Height 11 hands.
Colour dark chestnut.
Physique light frame, full mane and tail and good conformation.

Gelderland

Gelderland

Warmblood
Origin Gelderland.
Height 15.1 hands.
Colour chestnut, or grey.
Physique plain head,
almost convex profile,
crested neck, short-
coupled with a high set
tail.

Features extravagant
action and great presence.
Temperament docile,
good tempered and active.
Use carriage work, light
agricultural work and
riding.

Andalusian

Oldenburg

Anglo-
Norman

East
Friesian

Hackney

Gelderland

Gotland

Pony
Origin Gotland Islands,
Sweden.
Height 12.1 hands.
Colour dun, black, brown
or chestnut.
Physique light frame,
small straight head, long
back and low-set tail.

Features hardy, active.
Temperament gentle and
easy to handle, but can be
obstinate.
Use light agricultural
work, trotting races, as a
children's pony.

Tarpan

Little
Oriental

Gotland

Hackney Horse

Groningen

Warmblood
Origin Groningen, Holland.
Height 15.3 hands.
Colour dark colours.
Physique straight profile, long ears, deep powerful body and high-set tail.
Features frugal with a

stylish action.
Temperament gentle, obedient and willing.
Use light draught, riding and driving.

Friesian
Oldenburg
Groningen

Hackney

Warmblood and Pony
Origin UK.

Height horse, 15.1 hands; pony, under 14.2 hands.
Colour dark colours.
Physique smallish head, strong straightish shoulder, powerful hind quarters and tail set and carried high.
Features high stepping action.
Temperament spirited,

alert, vigorous.

Hackney
Horse
Fell
Dales
Hackney Pony

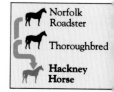

Norfolk
Roadster
Thoroughbred
Hackney Horse

Hanoverian

lflinger

y
gin The Tirol, Austria.
ght 14 hands.
our chestnut with
en mane and tail.
sique head tapers to
zle, broad chest, deep
h, long, broad back
short legs.

Features frugal, tough,
sure-footed and long-
lived.
Temperament docile,
good tempered, adaptable
and hard working.
Use mountain pony, riding
driving and pack work.

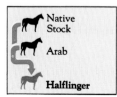

Hanoverian

Warmblood
Origin Hanover and
Lower Saxony, W.
Germany.
Height 16 hands.
Colour solid colours.
Physique powerful.
Features athletic.
Temperament intelligent,

courageous and versatile.
Use competition and
riding horse.

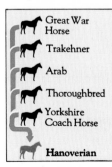

77

Highland

Hessen, Rheinlander

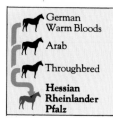

German Warm Bloods

Arab

Throughbred

Hessian Rheinlander Pfalz

Warmblood
Origin W. Germany.
Height 16 hands.
Physique strongly built.
Features good action.
Temperament good-tempered and adaptable.
Use riding.

Highland

Pony
Origin Western Isles and Scottish mainland.
Height mainland (Garron).
14.2 hands; islands (Western Isles), 13.2 hands.
Colour mainland, black or brown varying to dun and grey; islands, dun with a dorsal stripe, usually with black points and silver mane and tail.
Physique mainland, short ears, powerful loins, strong, short legs with feather tufts and full mane and tail; islands, smaller and finer.
Features strength.
Temperament intelligent, docile, sensitive and responsive.
Use mainland, deer stalking and work for crofters; islands, as children's pony.

Celtic Pony
Galloway
Arab
Highland Western Isles

Celtic Pony
Arab
French
Galloway
Clydesdale
Highland Garron

Hispano Anglo-Arab

Warmblood
Origin Estramadura and Andalusia, Spain.
Height 15.3 hands.
Colour bay, chestnut or grey.
Physique Arab features.
Features quick and nimble.
Temperament brave and intelligent.
Use competitions, riding, and testing young bulls.

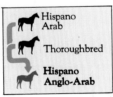

Hispano Arab
Thoroughbred
Hispano Anglo-Arab

Hokaido (Hocaido)

Pony
Origin Japan.
Height 13.1 hands.
Colour black, brown, bay or dun.
Physique like the Mongolian — thickset, short-coupled.
Features tough and strong.
Temperament adaptable and dependable.
Use general work pony.

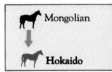

Mongolian
Hokaido

Holstein

Holstein

Warmblood
Origin Emsburg district of Holstein, W. Germany.
Height 16.1 hands.
Colour black, bay or brown.
Physique heavy frame with a strong, muscular neck and deep girth.

Features good action.
Temperament intelligent, obedient, good-tempered and spirited.

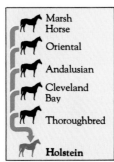

Marsh Horse
Oriental
Andalusian
Cleveland Bay
Thoroughbred
Holstein

Huzul

Pony
Origin Carpathian mountains, Poland.
Height 13.2 hands.
Colour dun or bay.
Physique Tarpan head and robust body.
Features tough and frugal.

Temperament willing, good-tempered.
Use pack and agricultural

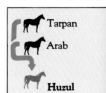

Tarpan
Arab
Huzul

Iceland

eland Pony

friendly, but independent.
Use mining, pack and
communication.

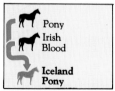

ay
gin Iceland.
ght 12.2 hands.
our grey, dun.
ysique stocky, compact
dy, full mane and tail.
ttures tough, able to
ble.
mperament docile and

81

Irish Draught

Iomud

Warmblood
Origin Central Asia.
Height 14 hands.
Colour grey, chestnut or bay.
Physique like the Akhal Teké but more compact.
Features great stamina, although not as fast as the Akhal Teké.

Temperament adaptable, courageous and enduring.
Use riding and racing.

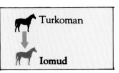

Irish Draught

Coldblood/Warmblood
Origin Ireland.
Height 16 hands.
Colour bay, brown or grey.
Physique straight face, short, muscular neck, longish back, strong, sloping hindquarters, good bone, little feather

and large round feet.
Features good jumper.
Temperament quiet, sensible, willing and active.
Use multi-purpose, but mainly breeding riding horses.

Irish Halfbred

ish Halfbred

Use riding.

Irish
Draught

Thoroughbred

Connemara

**Irish
Halfbred**

armblood
rigin Ireland.
eight 16.1 hands.
olour most colours.
ysique varies.
atures strong and
hletic.
mperament intelligent,
ld, sensible and
during.

83

Italian Heavy Draught

Italian Heavy Draught

Coldblood
Origin Northern and
Central Italy.
Height 15.2 hands.
Colour sorrel or roan.
Physique fine, long head
shortish neck, flat back
and powerful

hindquarters.
Features fast and strong.
Temperament active,
willing, kind and docile.
Use meat and agricultural
work.

84

Java

ava

Origin Java.
Height 12.2.
Colour most colours.
Physique strong frame.
Features ugly but strong
and tireless.
Temperament willing and
good worker.
Use pulling 'sados' (two-

wheeled taxis).

ony

Jutland

Coldblood
Origin Jutland Island,
Denmark.
Height 15.3 hands.
Colour chestnut or roan.
Physique massive,
compact horse, plain head
and short, feathered legs.
Features easy to handle.

Temperament kind,
gentle.
Use draught.

85

Karabakh

Kabardin

Warmblood
Origin Northern
Caucasus, USSR.
Height 15 hands.
Colour bay or black.
Physique sturdy frame,
short legs and long,
straight back.
Features sure-footed,
tough and long-lived.

Temperament calm,
intelligent and
independent.
Use mountain work as
pack or riding horse, local
equestrian games and
racing.

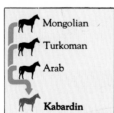

Mongolian
Turkoman
Arab
Kabardin

arabair

armblood
igin Uzbekistan, USSR.
ight 15.2 hands.
lour bay, chestnut, or
ey.
ysique similar to the
ab, but stouter. Two
es — the Saddle, which
fast and elegant and the
arness, which is larger
th a longer back.
atures ancient
ountain breed, tough
d versatile.
mperament sensible,
ave, intelligent and
sponsive.
e agricultural work,
ling and local sports.

Mongolian
Arab
Karabair

arabakh

armblood
igin Karabakh
ountains, Azerbaidzhan,
SSR.
ight 14.2 hands.
lour dun, bay or
estnut with metallic
een.
ysique tough mountain

horse with a small fine
head, low-set tail and good
feet.
Features ancient breed,
energetic and tough.
Temperament active and
sensible.
Use riding, equestrian
games and racing.

Persian
Turkoman
Arab
Karabakh

Karacabey

Warmblood
Origin Turkey.
Height 16 hands.
Colour solid colours.
Physique tough.
Features good quality
dual-purpose horse.
Temperament reliable.
Use riding, light draught,
agricultural work, cavalry
and pack.

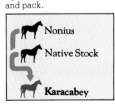

Nonius
Native Stock
Karacabey

Kathiawari

Pony
Origin Kathiawar
province, India.
Height 14.2 hands.
Colour most colours.
Physique light and

narrow, with some Arab
features.
Features frugal and tough
with great stamina.
Temperament uncertain
temper, enduring.
Use pack, transport and
riding.

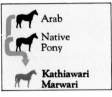

Arab
Native
Pony
**Kathiawari
Marwari**

Kazakh

Pony
Origin Kazakh, USSR.
Height 13 hands.
Colour bay, chestnut or
grey.
Physique similar to the
Mongolian.
Features tough; some
ponies amble rather than
walk.

Mongolian
Wild Horse
Don
Kazakh

Temperament willing and
enduring.
Use riding and herding,
milk and meat.

Kladruber

Kladruber

Warmblood
Origin Kladruby,
Czechoslovakia.
Height 16.2 hands.
Colour grey.
Physique larger version of
Andalusian.
Features superb carriage
horse.
Temperament proud,

obedient, intelligent and
good tempered.
Use agriculture and
harness.

Andalusian

Anglo-
Norman

Hanoverian

Oldenburg

Kladruber

Knabstrup

nabstrup

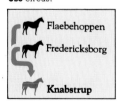

Temperament active, tractable and willing.
Use circus.

Flaebehoppen

Fredericksborg

Knabstrup

armblood
igin Denmark.
ight 15.3 hands.
lour spotted, Appaloosa
tterns on roan base.
ysique similar to, but
hter than, the
edericksborg.
atures distinctive
otted patterning.

Konik

Konik

Pony
Origin Poland.
Height 13.1 hands.
Colour yellow, grey or
blue dun, usually with
dorsal stripe.
Physique similar to the
Huzul.
Features long-lived,
frugal, hardy; the
foundation stock for many
Polish and Russian breeds.
Temperament
independent, but willing
and good tempered.
Use agricultural work for
lowland farmers.

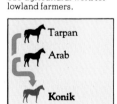

Landais

Pony
Origin the Landes region
of France.
Height 13.2 hands.
Colour dark colours.
Physique varies — usually
fine frame with an Arab-
like head.
Features frugal.
Temperament semi-wild.

Use riding and driving.

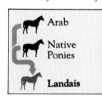

Lipizzaner

Warmblood
Origin Austria.
Height 15.1 hands.
Colour grey.
Physique largish head,

Lipizzaner

...all ears, crested neck,
...mpact body, short,
...ong legs and full, fine
...ne and tail.
...**atures** athletic, late to
...ature.
...**mperament** excellent
...intelligent, willing and
...edient.
...**e** high school equitation
...d driving.

Arab

Barb

Andalusian

Danish

German

Italian

Lipizzaner

Lithuanian and Latvian

Heavy Draught
Coldblood
Origin Baltic States,
USSR.
Height 15.3 hands.
Colour bay, black or
chestnut with flaxen mane
and tail.
Physique large head,
strong, long neck, sloping
bifurcated croup and little
feather.
Features free, straight
action, strong.
Temperament good
worker, but inclined to be
lazy.
Use draught.

Zemaituka

Oldenburg

Finnish
Draught

Swedish
Ardennes

**Lithuanian
and Latvian**

Llanero

Llanero

Warmblood
Origin Venezuela.
Height 14 hands.
Colour dun, yellow with
dark mane and tail, white
and yellow cream or pinto.
Physique lighter frame
than the Criollo; head
similar to Barb.
Features tough.

Temperament courageous
and enduring.
Use ranch work and
transport.

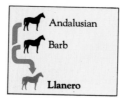

Lokai

Warmblood
Origin Uzbekistan, USSR.
Height 14.3 hands.
Colour grey, bay or
chestnut, often with
golden tint.
Physique varies, but
usually sturdy frame with
tough hooves; hair may be
curly.

Features a strong, sure
footed mountain horse.
Temperament tractable
willing and brave.
Use riding, pack, local
equestrian sports.

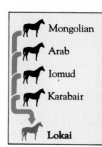

Mangalarga

sitana

mblood
gin Southern and
tral Portugal.
ght 15.1 hands.
ur grey.
sique small head,
l ears, large eyes,
k neck, short-coupled,
set tail and long legs.
tures frugal, hardy.

Temperament intelligent,
responsive, obedient and
brave.
Use cavalry, and in the
bullring.

Mangalarga

Warmblood
Origin Meiras Gerais,
Brazil.
Height 15 hands.
Colour grey, sorrel, roan
or bay.
Physique longish head,
short back, powerful
hindquarters, low set tail
and long legs.

Features hardy; gait
called 'marcha', between a
canter and a trot.
Temperament intelligent
and enduring, good riding
horse.
Use riding and ranch
work.

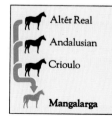

Altér Real
Andalusian
Crioulo
Mangalarga

93

Manipur

Manipur

Pony
Origin India.
Height 12 hands.
Colour most colours.
Physique thickset with high-set tail.
Features quick and manoeuvrable.
Temperament specialised

polo pony.
Use riding and polo.

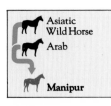

Asiatic Wild Horse
Arab
Manipur

Marwari

Pony.
Origin Marwar province of India.
Height 14.2 hands.
Colour most colours.
Physique light and narrow with some Arab features.
Features frugal and

tough, great stamina.
Temperament tough and enduring, but uncertain temper.
Use pack, transport and riding.

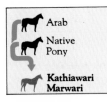

Arab
Native Pony
Kathiawari Marwari

Mecklenburg

Warmblood
Origin E. Germany.
Height 16 hands.
Colour solid colours.

Physique medium hea⟨ strong neck, compact body, powerful shoulde and loins.
Features like a slightly smaller Hanoverian.
Temperament willing, bold, kind and tractabl⟨
Use riding, cavalry.

Mongolian Wild Horse

Hanoverian

Mecklenburg

Missouri Foxtrotting

Warmblood
Origin Tennessee, USA.
Height 15.2 hands.
Colour sorrel.
Physique compact, strong body, long neck and intelligent head tapering to muzzle.
Features broken gait called 'foxtrot', walking with forelegs and trotting with hindlegs, at speeds of 10 to 15 mph.
Temperament good temper, enduring, stamina.
Use riding and stock work.

Mongolian Wild Horse

(Asiatic Wild Horse, equus przewalski poliakov).
Pony
Origin Mongolia.
Height 13.1 hands.
Colour black, brown, bay or dun.
Physique thickset, short-coupled, good bone.
Features tough, frugal, great stamina, fast over short distances.
Temperament very enduring, brave.
Use work pony of nomadic tribes; mares provide milk for cheese and a drink called *kumiss*.

Foreign Stock

Asiatic Wild Horse

Mongolian

Morgan

Morgan

Warmblood
Origin Massachusetts, USA.
Height 15 hands.
Colour bay, brown, black, or chestnut.
Physique short, broad head, thick neck, strong shoulders, back and hind quarters, good bone and full mane and tail.
Features versatile, tough high action.
Temperament kind, independent, active and hard working.
Use riding and driving.

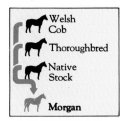

96

Murakosi

Murakosi

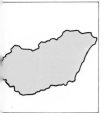

oldblood.
Origin Hungary.
Height 16 hands.
Colour chestnut, with
flaxen mane and tail.
Physique strong frame,
little wither, dip in back,
round hindquarters and
little feather.

Features strong and
active.
Temperament docile and
willing.
Use general draught and
agricultural work.

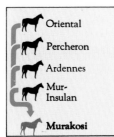

Murghese

Warmblood.
Origin Italy.
Height 15.2 hands.
Physique Oriental features but heavier frame.
Features versatile.
Temperament high-quality, good tempered.
Use dual-purpose horse for agricultural work or riding.

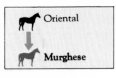

Mustang

Warmblood
Origin western states of America and Mexico.
Height 14.2 hands.
Colour most colours.
Physique sturdy, tough lightweight frame, good bone and tough feet.
Features hardy and frugal.
Temperament brave and independent, can be stubborn.
Use riding, showing, trail riding, endurance trials, competitions and stock work.

Native Tibetan (Nanfan)

Pony
Origin Tibet.
Height 12.2. hands.
Colour all colours.
Physique sturdy frame.
Features energetic and tough.
Temperament intelligent, active and courageous.
Use riding and general work.

New Forest

Pony
Origin New Forest, Hampshire, UK.
Height 12-14.2 hands.
Colour solid colours.
Physique great variety — type A, lighter, under 13.2 hands; type B, heavier, between 13.2 and 14.2 hands.
Features hardy, frugal.
Temperament brave, intelligent and willing. Very friendly and quick to learn, makes a safe and ideal children's pony.
Use riding.

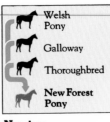

Nonius

Warmblood
Origin Hungary.
Height large Nonius, over 15.3 hands; small Nonius, under 15.3 hands.
Physique elegant head, long neck, strong back.
Features versatile, long-lived and active.
Temperament willing, consistent, calm, kind.
Use riding and agricultural work.

Noriker (South German Coldblood)

Coldblood
Origin Austria and Germany.
Height 16.1 hands.
Colour chestnut, bay, sometimes spotted.
Physique largish head, short, thick neck, straight shoulder, broad back and short legs with little feather.
Features sure-footed with a good action.
Temperament reliable.
Use agricultural and mountain work.

Novokirghiz

Warmblood.
Origin Kirghiz and Kazakhstan, USSR.
Height 15 hands.
Colour bay, chestnut or grey.

98

Oldenburg

ysique long neck, long
aight back, sloping
up, short legs.
atures tough, sure-
ted and frugal.
mperament strong and
during.
e mountain work —
rness and saddle;
vides milk.

Kirghiz

Don

Thoroughbred

Novokirghiz

Oldenburg

Warmblood
Origin Oldenburg and
East Friesland, W.
Germany.
Height 16.3 hands.
Physique largest of the
German warmbloods,
plain straight head, strong
shoulder, deep girth,
relatively short legs.

Features matures early.
Temperament bold, kind,
sensible.
Use riding and driving.

Andalusian

Barb

Hanoverian

Cleveland
Bay

Thoroughbred

Anglo-
Norman

Oldenburg

Orlov Trotter

Orlov Trotter

Warmblood
Origin USSR.
Height 16 hands.
Colour grey, black or bay.
Physique thickset, upright shoulder, broad chest, deep girth and long straight back.
Features active and fast.
Temperament bold and courageous.
Use trotting races, riding, harness.

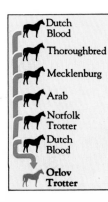

Dutch Blood

Thoroughbred

Mecklenburg

Arab

Norfolk Trotter

Dutch Blood

Orlov Trotter

Pahlavan

Warmblood
Origin Iran.
Height 15.2-16 hands.
Colour solid colours.
Physique strong and elegant.
Features developed by crossing Plateau Persian with Arab and Thoroughbred.
Temperament spirited.
Use riding.

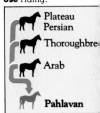

Plateau Persian

Thoroughbred

Arab

Pahlavan

100

Palomino

alomino

Warmblood
Origin California, USA.
Height 14 hands.
Colour golden with no
markings other than white
n face or below the knees;
mane and tail white, silver,
r ivory; dark eyes.
Physique varies;
egistered for colour, so

does not yet breed true to
type.
Features distinctive
colouration.
Temperament intelligent,
good general-purpose
horse.
Use riding, driving and
stock work.

Paso Fino

Warmblood
Origin Puerto Rico.
Height 14.3 hands.
Colour most colours.
Physique Arab-like head,
strong back, loins and
quarters and hard legs,
which are light of bone.
Features spirited; extra
four-beat gaits, of which

the slowest is the *paso fino*,
then the *paso corto* and the
paso largo.
Temperament alert,
tractable and willing.
Use riding.

Spanish

Peruvian
Stepping Horse

Paso Fino

101

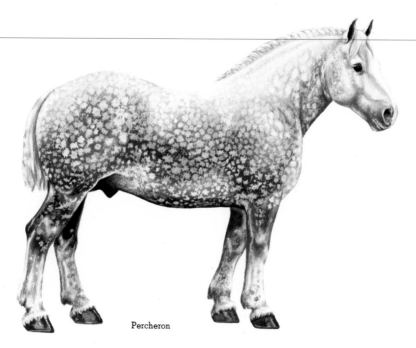

Percheron

Peneia

Pony
Origin Peneia,
Peloponnese, Greece.
Height 10-14 hands.
Colour most colours.
Physique Oriental.
Features frugal and
hardy.
Temperament willing.

Use pack and agricultural
work.

Percheron

Coldblood.
Origin France.
Height 16.1 hands.
Colour grey or black.
Physique Oriental-type
head, strong, well-
proportioned body, full
mane and tail, clean, hard
legs without feather.
Features good action and

great presence.
Temperament energetic,
intelligent and docile.
Use draught.

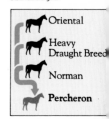

Persian Arab

Persian Arab.

Temperament spirited
and intelligent.
Use riding, and improving
other breeds.

Thoroughbred.
Origin Iran.
Height 15 hands.
Colour grey or bay.
Physique elegant,
compact body, otherwise
as Arab.
Features possibly older
than the desert Arab.

Peruvian Stepping Horse

Peruvian Stepping Horse

Warmblood
Origin Peru.
Height 15 hands.
Colour bay or chestnut.
Physique broad chest.
short-coupled, and strong
round hindquarters.
Features endurance and a
special extended gait,
similar to an amble.
Temperament enduring,
thrives under stress.
Use riding and stock work.

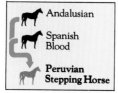

Andalusian

Spanish Blood

Peruvian Stepping Horse

Pindos

Pony
Origin mountains of
Thessaly and Epirus,
Greece.
Height 12.1 hands.
Colour grey or dark
colours.
Physique tough, light
frame.
Features mountain pony,
mares often used to breed
mules.
Temperament hardy.
Use riding and light
agricultural work.

Oriental

Ancient Stock

Pindos

Pinto

Pinto

Temperament intelligent
and enduring.
Use ranch work riding,
showing.

Warmblood
Origin USA.
Height varies.
Colour black with white or
white with any colour but
black.
Physique varies.
Features colour breed,
traditionally associated
with American Indians.

Plateau Persian

Warmblood
Origin Central Persian Plateau.
Height 15 hands.
Colour grey, bay or chestnut.
Physique Arab features, but this varies as it is an amalgamation of separate breeds.
Features good action, strong and sure-footed.
Temperament has fire and character.
Use riding.

Arab
Shiragazi
Quashquai
Darashouri
Basseri
Bahhtiari
Jaf
Plateau Persian

Pleven

Warmblood
Origin Bulgaria.
Height 15.2 hands.
Colour chestnut.
Physique sturdier version of the Arab.
Features robust.
Temperament kind, brave, intelligent and spirited.
Use all-purpose.

Local Arab
Hungarian Gidran Arab
Strelets Anglo-Arab
Gidran Anglo-Arab
Local Anglo Arab
Pleven

Poitevin

Coldblood
Origin Poitiers, France.
Height 16.3 hands.
Colour dun.
Physique plain conformation, large head, long body, big feet with heavy feather.
Features docile.
Temperament relatively unintelligent and can be lethargic.
Use mares put to Baudet Poitevins (jackasses of about 16 hands), to breed large mules.

Norwegian
Danish
Dutch
Poitevin

Polish Arab

Warmblood
Origin Poland.
Height 14.3 hands.
Colour grey, chestnut or bay.
Physique similar to the Arab, but with more sloping quarters and tail carried lower.
Temperament like Arab, bold, spirited, intelligent.
Use racing, breeding and riding.

Pony of the Americas

Pony
Origin USA.
Height 12.1 hands.
Colour Appaloosa patterns.
Physique Arab-like head, short back and round body.
Features smooth, free action.
Temperament willing, gentle and versatile, ideal as children's pony.

Shetland Pony
Appaloosa
Pony of the Americas

Quarter Horse

Quarter-Horse

Warmblood
Origin USA.
Height 15.3 hands.
Colour solid colours, usually chestnut.
Physique short head, powerful, short-coupled body, large round hindquarters and fine legs.
Features fast and versatile.
Temperament intelligent, sensible, active and nimble.
Use riding, racing, ranch work and rodeos.

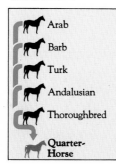

Arab

Barb

Turk

Andalusian

Thoroughbred

Quarter-Horse

Rhineland Heavy Draught
(Rhenish-German)

Coldblood
Origin W. Germany.
Height 16.1 hands.
Colour chestnut or chestnut roan with flaxen mane and tail.
Physique heavy and compact with short, feathered legs.
Features strength, early maturity.
Temperament obliging, mature and good-tempered.
Use draught.

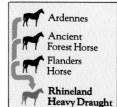

Ardennes

Ancient Forest Horse

Flanders Horse

Rhineland Heavy Draught

Saddlebred

Russian Heavy Draught

Coldblood
Origin Ukraine, USSR.
Height 14.2 hands.
Colour chestnut, bay or roan.
Physique the smallest coldblood; thickset, massive neck, broad back

and sloping croup.
Features strong active and fast.
Temperament good-tempered and lively.
Use agricultural work.

Swedish Ardennes

Percheron

Orlov Trotter

Indigenous Ukraine stock

Russian Heavy Draught

Russian Trotter

Warmblood.
Origin USSR.
Height 15.3 hands.
Colour black, bay or chestnut.
Physique mixture of Orlov and Standard-bred characteristics.
Features faster than the Orlov.
Temperament like the

Orlov Trotter

Standardbred

Russian Trotter

Orlov — active, bold and courageous.
Use trotting races.

Saddlebred

Warmblood
Origin USA.
Height 15.2 hands.
Colour black, brown, bay grey or chestnut.
Physique small head wit

Salerno

...ight profile. Strong
...y and hindquarters,
...carried artificially
...h.
...**tures** five gaited
...on, three normal gaits
...s a four-beat rack, at
...ch it can reach 30
...h.
...**perament** great
...sence, gentle and
sweet temper.
Use showing, riding and
driving.

| Narrangansett Pacer |
| Morgan |
| Thoroughbred |
| **Saddlebred** |

Salerno

Warmblood
Origin Meremma and
Salerno, Italy.
Height 16 hands.
Colour solid colours.
Physique large, refined
head and good
conformation.
Features aristocratic,

quality saddle horse.
Temperament intelligent
responsive and gentle.
Use riding, especially
army.

| Neapolitan |
| **Salerno** |

109

Schleswig Heavy Draught

Sandalwood

Pony
Origin Indonesia.
Height 13 hands.
Colour dun with dorsal
stripe, dark mane and tail.
Physique lighter frame,
finer coat and more
elegant than other
Indonesian ponies.

Features fast.
Temperament hard-
working and enduring.
Use bareback racing and
general work.

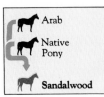

Schleswig Heavy Draught

Coldblood.
Origin W. Germany.
Height 15.2-16 hands.
Colour chestnut, flaxen
mane and tail.
Physique similar to the
Jutland — plain, close-
coupled, little feather.

Features active, good
mover.
Temperament kind,
gentle and willing.
Use draught.

Shagya Arab

elle Francais

rmblood
gin Northern France.
ight 16 hands.
lour solid colours.
ysique robust frame,
werful shoulder, strong
gish back, deep girth
i powerful
dquarters.

Features athletic.
Temperament brave,
calm and good-tempered.
Use riding and
competitions.

Shagya Arab

Warmblood
Origin Hungary.
Height 15 hands.
Colour grey.
Physique Arab features.
small head.
Features hardy, frugal
and active.
Temperament versatile,

alert and intelligent.
Use cavalry, general
riding and driving.

111

Shetland

Shetland

Pony
Origin Shetland and
Orkney Islands, UK.
Height 9.3 hands (6.2
hands the smallest yet
recorded).
Colour black, brown or
coloured.
Physique small head, face

usually concave, small
ears, short, strong back,
full mane and tail; winter
coat very thick, summer
coat fine and sleek.
Features hardy and
strong; can pull loads
twice its own weight.
Temperament very gentle
and courageous, easy to
train.
Use mining, general work,
driving and riding.

Celtic
Pony

**Shetland
Pony**

Shire

ire

dblood
gin central counties,

ght 17 hands.
our dark with white
kings.
sique face nearly
vex, broad forehead,
, crested neck, broad
k, sloping croup and

much fine silky feather.
Features strength; the
tallest breed in the world.
Temperament docile and
gentle, active, industrious
and adaptable.
Use pack, agricultural
work and riding.

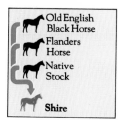

Skyros

Skyros

Pony
Origin Island of Skyros, Greece.
Height 10 hands.
Colour dun, brown or grey.
Physique light bone, upright shoulder, often cow-hocked.

Features an ancient breed; Greece's smallest pony.
Temperament tough work pony.
Use pack, carrying water, agricultural work and riding.

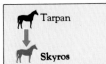

Sokolsky

Warmblood
Origin Poland.
Height 15.2 hands.
Colour chestnut, brown or grey.
Physique large head, sturdy frame, short, straight back, short legs and large round feet with

little feather.
Features frugal.
Temperament kind, ca
patient and hard-worki
Use agricultural work.

Standardbred

orraia

ny
gin River Sorraia
trict, Portugal.
ght 13 hands.
our dun, with a dorsal
pe and stripes on legs.
ysique primitive
pearance, long head,
aight profile, long ears,
n neck and straight

back.
Features tough and
frugal.
Temperament enduring.
Use runs wild.

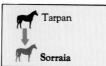

Spiti
Pony
Origin India.
Height 12 hands.
Colour grey.
Physique thickset and
short-coupled.
Features sure-footed and
tough.
Temperament intelligent,

alert and tireless, but not
always good-tempered.
Use transportation in
mountains.

Standardbred

Warmblood
Origin USA.
Height 15.2 hands.
Colour solid colours.
Physique varies as it is
bred for speed; usually
muscular Thoroughbred
type with longer back,
short legs and powerful

115

Suffolk Punch

shoulders.
Features stamina, speed.

Thoroughbred

Canadian Trotter

Hackney

Narrangansett Pacer

Arab

Barb

Morgan

Standardbred

Temperament bold, active, brave and enduring.
Use driving and racing.

Suffolk Punch

Coldblood
Origin east Anglia, UK.
Height 16.1 hands.
Colour chestnut, with no white markings.
Physique short clean legs, massive neck and shoulders, square body.
Features good action, frugal and long-lived.

Temperament kind, active and intelligent.
Use draught.

Native Great Horse

Norfolk Trotter

Norfolk Cob

Flanders Horse

Suffolk Punch

116

Sumba

Sumba

Use dancing and general work.

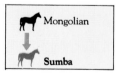

ony
rigin Indonesia.
eight 12.2 hands.
olour dun with dorsal
ripe, dark mane and tail.
ysique primitive type.
atures special use as a
ncing pony.
mperament tough,
lling and intelligent.

Swedish Halfbred

Swedish Ardennes

Coldblood
Origin Sweden.
Height 15.3 hands.
Colour black, brown, bay or chestnut.
Physique similar to, but smaller than, the Belgian Ardennes.
Features active.

Temperament energetic, quiet and kindly.
Use agricultural work and timber hauling.

Ardennes

Swedish Horse

Swedish Ardennes

Swedish Halfbred

Warmblood
Origin Sweden.
Height 16.1 hands.
Colour any solid colour.
Physique smallish, intelligent head, large bold eye, longish neck, deep girth and straightish back.
Features extravagant, straight action.
Temperament intelligent, bold, sensible and obedient.
Use general riding and competitions.

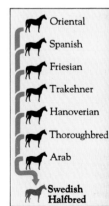

Oriental

Spanish

Friesian

Trakehner

Hanoverian

Thoroughbred

Arab

Swedish Halfbred

Tarpan

wiss Halfbred

armblood
rigin Switzerland.
eight 16.1 hands.
olour any solid colour.
ysique well-made,
rong horse.
atures athletic, with a
od action.
mperament good-

tempered and versatile.
Use riding and driving.

Thoroughbred

Anglo-
Norman

Holstein

Trakehner

Hanoverian

Swedish
Halfbred

**Swiss
Halfbred**

Tarpan (equus przevalskii gmellini antonius)

Pony
Origin Poland.
Height 13 hands.
Colour brown or dun with dorsal stripe, dark mane and tail, and stripes on

forelegs and inner thighs; coat may change to white in winter.
Physique long head, longish ears, short neck longish back and fine legs.
Features tough and fertile.
Temperament independent, brave and tenacious.
Use exhibited in zoos and also roams wild.

Equus Celticus

Tarpan

119

Tennessee Walking Horse

Tennessee Walking Horse

Warmblood
Origin Tennessee, USA.
Height 15.2 hands.
Colour solid colours.
Physique common head, crested neck, strong, sloping shoulder, powerful loins and hindquarters,

clean legs and full mane and tail, carried artificially high.
Features running walk, with the forefeet raised high and the hind legs moving with long strides.

Narrangansett Pacer

Standardbred

Canadian Pacer

Saddlebred

Morgan

Tennessee Walking Horse

Temperament docile, kind willing and alert.
Use showing and riding.

Tersky

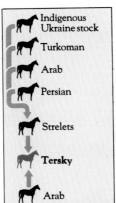

Indigenous
Ukraine stock

Turkoman

Arab

Persian

Strelets

Tersky

Arab

Warmblood
Origin Stavropol region,
USSR.
Height 15 hands.
Colour grey.
Physique Arab features.
Features three types,
light, medium and
thickset.
Temperament kind,

intelligent and enduring.
Use racing, competitions
and the circus.

Thoroughbred

Thoroughbred

Thoroughbred
Origin UK.
Height 16 hands.
Colour solid colours.
Physique varies from close-coupled sprinters with large, powerful hindquarters to big-framed, longer backed,

big-boned chasers. Must have an elegant head, long neck, sloping shoulder, prominent wither and silky coat.
Features fast and active.
Temperament bold, brave and spirited.

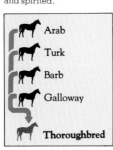

Use racing, riding and improving other breeds.

Timor

Pony
Origin Timor, Indonesia.
Height 11.1 hands.
Colour dark colours.
Physique fine but sturdy frame.

Features agile.
Temperament possesses common sense, willingness and endurance.
Use agricultural work an transportation.

Toric

Warmblood
Origin Estonia, USSR.

122

Trakehner

ght 15.1 hands.
our chestnut or bay.
sique long, muscular
ly, short strong legs
light feather.
tures great strength
stamina.
mperament good-
pered, calm and hard
king.
light draught.

Klepper
Thoroughbred
Trakehner
Orlov
Trotter
Hanoverian
Ardennes
Hackney
East
Friesian

Toric

Trakehner (East Prussian)

Warmblood
Origin East Prussia.
Height 16.1 hands.
Colour dark colours.
Physique head is broad
between the eyes, tapering
to the muzzle; long

straight neck, prominent
withers, deep girth and
flattish hind quarters.
Features extravagant
action.
Temperament intelligent,
active, good-tempered
and loyal.
Use competitions and
riding.

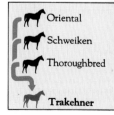

Oriental
Schweiken
Thoroughbred

Trakehner

Vladimir Heavy Draught

Turkoman
(Turkmen)

Warmblood
Origin Iran.
Height 15.2 hands.
Colour solid colours.
Physique narrow chest,
light but tough frame.
Features floating action

and speed.
Temperament enduring.
Use foundation stock for
other breeds, riding,
cavalry and racing.

Mongols'
Horse

Scythians'
Horse

Turkoman

Viatka

Pony
Origin Viatsky territory —
Baltic States, USSR.
Height 13.2 hands.
Colour dark, sometimes
with dorsal stripe.
Physique plain head,
sturdy frame, broad,
straight back, short legs

with good bone.
Features frugal, tough
and fast.
Temperament obedien
Use all-purpose pony.

Native
Baltic Stock

Oriental
Stock

Klepper

Viatka

Konik

adimir Heavy aught

dblood
gin Vladimir district,
SR.
ight 16 hands.
lour any solid colour.
ysique strong frame,
od conformation, with
ther on legs.
atures active and
werful.
mperament energetic,
mpetitive and hard-
orking.
se draught.

Cleveland Bay
Suffolk Punch
Shire
Ardennes
Percheron
Vladimir Heavy Draught

Velsh Cob
Section D)

Warmblood
Origin Wales, UK.
Height 14-15.1 hands.
Colour solid colours.
Physique compact, great substance, quality head, strong shoulder, deep, powerful back and silky feather.
Features strength, stamina; high knee action.
Temperament bold, equable intelligent and energetic.
Use all purpose; driving and riding.

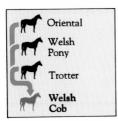

Oriental
Welsh Pony
Trotter
Welsh Cob

Welsh Mountain
(Section A)

Pony
Origin Wales, UK.
Height under 12 hands.
Colour grey, brown or chestnut.
Physique Arab-like head, long, crested neck, sloping shoulder, short back and high set tail.
Features great endurance.
Temperament intelligent, high-spirited and courageous.
Use riding, foundation stock for children's riding ponies.

Welsh Pony
(Section B)

Pony
Origin Wales, UK.
Height 12-13.2 hands.
Colour solid colours.
Physique larger version of Section A.
Features good action.
Temperament intelligent, high-spirited, kind, good children's pony.
Use riding.

Welsh Mountain Pony
Welsh Cob
Thoroughbred
Welsh Pony

Welsh Pony

Welsh Pony
(Section C)

Pony
Origin Wales, UK.
Height under 13.2 hands.
Colour solid colours.
Physique cob type, with
silky feather.
Features hardy, active
and frugal.

Temperament stout-
hearted.
Use driving and trekking.

Westphalian

Warmblood
Origin Westphalia,
W. Germany.
Height 16.1 hands.
Colour any solid colour.

Physique similar to the
Hanoverian.
Features developed from
the Hanoverian — good
general-purpose horse.
Temperament
courageous, intelligent
and versatile.
Use riding, competitions
and driving.

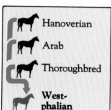

Hanoverian
Arab
Thoroughbred
West-
phalian

Wielkopolski

Warmblood
Origin Poland.
Height 16 hands.
Colour chestnut or bay.
Physique a compact, wel
proportioned horse.
Features formed by
amalgamating the
Masuren and Posnan.

126

Wielkopolski

Trakehner

Hanoverian

Thoroughbred

Konik

Poznan

Wielkopolski

Masuren

East
Prussian

Temperament excellent,
courageous and hard-
working.
Use riding competitions
and light draught.

Württemburg

Warmblood
Origin Württemburg,
W. Germany.

Height 16 hands.
Colour black, brown, bay
or chestnut.
Physique cob type —

Arab

Anglo-
Norman

Nonius

Oldenburg

Trakehner

Suffolk
Punch

Württemburg

straight profile to face,
deep girth, straight back
and good bone.
Features hardy, with great
stamina.
Temperament gentle,
hard-working and willing.
Use riding and driving.

127

Zemaituka
(Pechora)

Pony
Origin Baltic States, USSR.
Height 13.2 hands.
Colour brown, palomino or dun with dorsal stripe.
Physique straight face, smallish ears, short neck and straight back.
Features hardy and frugal.
Temperament good-tempered intelligent, willing and energetic.
Use riding and work.

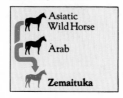

Asiatic Wild Horse

Arab

Zemaituka